Sweet REDEMPTION

JAMES THOMAS

ISBN 978-1-0980-4142-7 (paperback)
ISBN 978-1-0980-4143-4 (hardcover)
ISBN 978-1-0980-4144-1 (digital)

Copyright © 2020 by James Thomas

All rights reserved. No part of this publication may be reproduced, distributed, or transmitted in any form or by any means, including photocopying, recording, or other electronic or mechanical methods without the prior written permission of the publisher. For permission requests, solicit the publisher via the address below.

Christian Faith Publishing, Inc.
832 Park Avenue
Meadville, PA 16335
www.christianfaithpublishing.com

Printed in the United States of America

DEDICATION

This writing is dedicated to my beautiful wife Tanya who was born an Angel. This success story has materialized through trust, forgiveness, support and by us praying together daily. God led us out. Thank you for supporting the idea that a person can clear their mind by trusting in our Lord. I would not be the person I am without you. I have to give credit where credit is due, I give credit to you for helping me through. This is a miraculous journey, life altering with you. I love you dearly, thank you and this is my story, this is my song.

Foreword

Thank you, Lord, for bringing us to this day with a clear mind and blessings laid out before us. We cherish the mercy you have for us and the grace we walk in. Though we crawled, stumbled, and walked, we praise your name now even more now that we are able to run. We have been filled and are overflowing with your goodness that we can share and give back to a lost and dying world. From here out to eternity, we shall look beyond this world and know that our focus is to meet in heaven. The distractions are bygone because we handed our burdens here on earth over to you. We love you God and thank you for our clear, concise minds and ability to act accordingly to your word. The blessings are overflowing from our cup as we spill over with the joy you've placed in our hearts. We give you all. Amen.

This is a separate part of my life, the aftereffect or some would say these are the redemption years. God, thank you for helping me with wisdom, understanding, favor, and thank you even more for carrying my tiny burdens. Lord, I give you my life full of the joy you have filled me with. I am anxious to get out and make the world a better place, content that your hand is upon me and protects every step I take. Perfectly content in all I do, knowing you are not only beside me—you are in me. You are my God, my Savior, my Jesus, and my Spirit. I praise and worship your name and am grateful you called my name and wrote my name in the Book of Life for eternity. I will go where you want me to go this day, Lord, and do with your guidance what you have called me to do. Thank you for another day, and thank you for exceptional health.

Focus on Christ is my vision, not focusing on things that will distract us. I stay true to your word and am not hindered by little demons picking and tormenting that in which we have faith in God to take care of. Your word is true, and we walk our steps knowing we are secure in the palm of your hand. We can do what we are called to do, and that is to make this world a better place for future generations and for them to see what our progress in you lord can do not only for today but for tomorrow.

Thank you, Lord, for helping me to stay focused and watching over me as I walk in the joy of your Spirit. Thank you for helping me with favor in my learning ability. Thank you for giving me wisdom in small decision-making, and thank you for this fast I have been on. I lift up my marriage to you and pray for the best for the distant family that seems so elusive sometimes. I don't try to figure it out because again I know you have it because I give all to you, Lord. Amen.

There are so many years ahead to do good in this world. Thank you, Lord, for sweet redemption, for it is here.

Sweet Redemption Wandered Forty Years 1960's

In 1961, a child was born. From what I was told, I was carried through August and was supposed to be born by the end of August for sure. It makes me wonder why I did not want to come out of the womb. What was going on out there that I would not want to embrace the joys of this world? After reading this book, hopefully this question will be answered. April 9th was my mom's birthday, and if it weren't for that time in history, I would not be writing this book.

In early September, (around Labor Day weekend) little James Dwayne Thomas was born into Monroe, North Carolina, down from the Union Memorial Hospital, a couple of turns to Olive Branch Road. Olive Branch is symbolic in this because it has been a symbol of peace. Extending the Olive Branch means to end hostilities and end conflict. Keep this in mind while reading Sweet Redemption. There is also language about the dove and the Olive Brach which signifies new beginnings. How fitting for a troubled child like me that overcame the odds to have been raised on Olive Branch Road. I get it now. How would this instance change the world? Would it be for good or for bad? We'll start this venture by saying that I was the fifth of five boys born from 1955 until 1961. We were relatively close in age to our neighbors who had five boys as well. The brother before me was born in 1959.

In 1958, Mom gave birth to her third boy. He ended up being the middle child for whatever that is worth. Is there truth in the old saying that a middle child struggles with finding themselves? That is a whole different issue. I can't say he was crazy—we were all crazy, especially the two that were born before him.

Our neighbors just not even a quarter mile out the window had five boys too. We were borderline poverty, and they were poverty. After many years, Rachel, the mom, finally had a girl, then Rachel died of cancer. Their dad and my dad were alcoholics.

Ten boys, what could we do today? We would hike, build forts, camp, fight, and make heroic scenes as boys. We were tough, strong, and the lifestyle was hard, abusive in some eyes. Was it normal? Probably not. Was ten boys normal? By far not. Parents had to work and we were on our own.

Being a baby of five boys, I know from pictures, memories and past stories that I was tossed around, picked on, and manipulated by the older four. I also know I was babied and somewhat protected by our parents when they were home. We were the pure specimen of country-wannabe-city. We were like cats wanting out of their cages, to get out in the country to run. We were somewhat segregated from the world being born out in the county in the fifties and sixties. My wife was born in Tennessee in December 1958, so she was already digging into the cupboards by the time I opened my eyes to the world, she in Tennessee and me in North Carolina, looking to the same God. One of the very first memories I have is having either the chicken pox or measles. Still in a carrier, my mom backing up the car to the door and trying to keep me out of the sun. My point in this is that there was some responsibility and some natural love. I always remember that.

So where was Dad? Not at home, out working to help support a high-maintenance mom and five boys? Billy Joe was a child born on a farm, an only child. He had to work as a child; he went to school and worked. What did he do for fun? Probably went to the city of Monroe and shopped. So once he turned eighteen, he got married, him and his dad built a house next door to their house and started out from there on his own. He graduated and went into the police force. He was a greyhound bus driver later, and then, just guessing, the alcohol experience forced him into factory work. I don't know that for sure, but I testify that when my eyes came to light, he could drink a case of Pabst Blue Ribbon in a day. Liquor was a different story, it would make him throw up. Smoking was a whole different story as well. Second-hand smoke was rough. He smoked like a freight train. It was the abuse to his system that led him to an early grave at forty-two, fathom that, here I am nearing sixty. I remember when I went from forty-two to forty-three.

Mom was the older of two children. She had a little brother ten years younger. Boy-girl situation, I don't think they were that close. My mom was a school drop-out and did not graduate. She fell in love with my dad at a young age, and her dad was hard on her to keep her at home. I found a diary here she had at fifteen and sixteen years old. She had the love bug and wanted out to venture. She got out and then had the five boys before she was twenty-three or so. Moving through the 1950's and 1960's with five boys, fast times and alcohol in the mix was a good time just waiting to happen and it did, fast. My dad had the potential to lead, but it seemed alcohol was a major deterrent in success to keep him from being a policeman or a bus driver. I see pictures of jobs he had. He ended up a factory worker, alcoholic and smoker dying at such a young age. What a fast life. I just think it's so sad. My uncle ended up being a good-looking kid and went off to Vietnam. He learned how to repair siding on helicopters, sheet metal. He opened a body shop in Monroe later. Would he do it again? I doubt it, but it sounded like he learned something. My uncle battled his demons like us all but got saved in his later years. Later in life he lost a daughter (his first born) and her husband as well in a bad wreck. The daughter's sister and her husband took the three children and raised them with their two. This is a great family. My uncle did well, even better after he got saved. Psalm 121 is fitting for him where it talks about our help comes from the Lord. He is one of our last living relatives before us three brothers that are left. I have a few nieces and nephews although there is very little contact. I keep my door open though, never burn bridges. Isaiah 64:5 refers to how God helped me because I always tried to do right. I talked to God as a young child, probably about eight, when I realized what a stagnate situation it was. Later in life I said, "Here I am, Lord, use me," and off I went, it worked. I mean why wouldn't I? The options for survival were few in number.

So we were growing up and venturing out and one thing I remember early was things like when my grandma on my mom's side would race us home from her house in Wingate, North Carolina, we'd hit every stop sign and speed limit sign with rocks and bottles riding in the back of a truck. This was absolutely crazy. She'd drive like sixty-five with five kids in the back of a truck throwing rocks at signs and stuff like that. This kind of stuff was just the start of pushing the envelope.

My Grandma Thomas always baked pies for us hungry grandkids, and we'd have to walk down there and get them. Whenever the phone would ring, we would be like "you answer it, no, you answer it" knowing it was probably going to be one of those calls about needing to go down there and pick up some food. It was hard to get away from her without a lengthy conversation, so we'd argue about who had to go get the items. We argued about who had to pick up free food. It was about one hundred yards from our house. When the food arrived, it was a true blessing indeed. We ate our share of mayonnaise sandwiches when times were tough. Times when we would score a two-liter soda, we would line up four or five glasses and measure to make sure all five were evenly filled. We were afraid we might not get as much as the next brother. Now, looking back I see how hilarious that is. Some may consider it desperate. I have eaten polk salad as well. We worked on empty stomachs a lot. One time I was down behind the old chicken house stringing some barbed wire and somebody came around the corner and it sort of scared me. It was the one time in my life that I actually fainted. I wonder now, why did I faint? Was it because of lack of nourishment? I declare now that it was likely. Working in the hot sun, no food. The sudden scare made my knees collapse, will never forget that strange moment.

I was an honest child I remember because one time at my grandpa's work, I returned a dime to him in front of his coworkers and they all made a big deal out of it. He was proud that I was honest. I did have some good roots. I never forgot he was proud of me. After he died, I saw all the vultures come out of woodwork to practically kill, steal, and destroy what he had worked for all his life. I was too young to do anything about it.

On an odd note, my mom used to bathe in front of me, and my dad left nude pictures all around the house. It was terrible to have to figure sexuality out on my own. This had an effect on my social skills as a young man, and I would not recommend this mental spark on any young man. There have been books written about this subject and I stand with righteousness and good education about this subject. Education on this subject is crucial for the understanding and soundness for adolescents.

We had this one toy store in Monroe we'd raid every chance we got to go. We'd throw toys over aisles across the store. I think back and just wonder, how? We did not have much parenting and we would push it as far as we could. My point is that we were slightly out of control with not much hope because we were not taught to behave. By the time I was two, my future wife Tanya was getting into school and social behavior, starting her education. Tanya had a rough go when she was born. God gave her great parents and she adjusted into her lifestyle. There was an odd twist in her first few years, although she'd need to have the freedom to express those times of her life if she chooses. She talks about it from time to time. Her story makes me love her even more; we had a bit in common. I always thought the reason I was born so late is the fact that my family was so loud and boisterous. I was probably scared to enter this world. I wonder if Tanya heard loud noises when she was in the womb. This is strange talk, but I know babies hear what's going on and they either like it or they don't. It makes lasting impressions is my thought, although God does heal. I am living proof.

When I was learning to walk, and getting out of the crib, I have a couple of memories. Nightmares were frequent and very troubling to my mind I remember vividly. It is funny to look at some of the pictures of four older brothers and a baby. A lot of commotion going on and my parents worked. I learned to have the right attitude, and I learned to regain that good attitude whenever I lost it. My grandmother comes in to play here. The grandmother that lived next door, and she worked at home, looking after us, canning, and keeping the home while her husband was a meat cutter at a local market called five points. It was five roads that met at one point. I ended up living at Grandma's house a lot, especially after the older ones started school. I remember the brothers going off to school, and ever who had to spend the night at Grandma's house, they had to take some clothes, it is part of the memory. It was quite boring and probably more normal. She always kept a consistent attitude, pressing toward a goal. I believe their goal was to live under their means and have enough for themselves and to help the less fortunate, which was us kids. At two years old, I was at my grandma's house, standing in front of a black-and-white TV, when I saw the carriage take John F. Kennedy to the grave. I could tell my grandparents were torn apart, so I watched with them, not knowing, as the years went by, I would learn about Oswald and Ruby and the impact of JFK. I think it was seven years later when man landed on the moon. Obviously, John F. Kennedy was a true visionary at a young age. That was in November 1963, I was twenty-six months old. Then I went back to playing at Grandma's house. Tanya was five and already settling in good with her family at this point in time.

As I said, my dad was born on a farm and was likely a farmhand for the younger part of his life. My mom spoke of cotton fields and they were both born in the late thirties. I saw and walked through cotton fields but never had to pick the seeds out for money. I know it was hard to do because I did it just to see what it was all about. I heard such horror stories about picking cotton. I know it stunk. We grew up around my grandpa's farm with pigs, chicken, cows, bulls, tractors, making cider, butter and other necessities. We often smelled the scents in Grandma's kitchen, but the one memory was of apple fritters. They grew the apples, rolled the dough, and mashed the edges with a fork to make the rippled edges. These will never be made again. They also made some kind of toast with brown sugar and butter, cakes and lots of pies, churned butter, made cheese, fed off the chickens, pork and beef. We grew a lot of vegetables and canned beans, tomatoes, pumpkins, all the above, and water from the well. They leased some of the land for crops and hustled at the cattle sales. It was profitable because they bought a lot of land. On the farm we had a big hog pen and my grandpa was in manure up to his ankles one day when a hog stepped on his foot and he ended up losing a couple of toes due to gangrene. Right after that, I guess his heart gave out at work and he died at work while cutting meat. This was devastating. He was about sixty-two or something, and I had the utmost respect for him. It was at this point that I realized that people go away. I must've been six. It wasn't the first death. I lost my Great-grandpa in his sleep that I was named after, and my great-grandma died in the same room I was in when I was young. She was just sitting there on the couch while I was playing on the floor and her head fell back. She went to sleep right in front of me and did not wake up. My grandma was like "I think she just passed". She had died like right there, peacefully. When my grandpa died, I could see the emptiness in my grandmother's life, it was very sad. The death of my grandpa was a sad thing to our family when I was a child because we needed his sane presence of mind and some would say "his leadership". It was the hollow feeling that only God can fill. You look out and see emptiness. You look out and see Grandma now forced to walk blindly into the future, and she ends up years later getting beaten down by her own grandson. She had a godly attitude, but the ruthlessness (Ruth and Naomi) of our fellowman sometimes is beyond anything I can fathom. I have seen how low people can be and I retain a heart for the less fortunate.

 Some of those memories back on the farm are strange to think back on now after all the places and things I have learned. My grandma told me one day she would show me how to collect the eggs, so we went down to the chicken house and entered. There was straw and water cans that fill the pails as they drink. We threw some food in the pails, and there was this big gray metal chicken coup that hung on the wall. The chickens would sit in each cubbyhole and lay their eggs there. I'd have to stand on a crate and reach my hand in each one and get any eggs found. The scary part was that she said you might grab a snake every once in a while, but they were only black snakes and they won't hurt you. I'll be honest with you. I saw snakes down there eight to ten feet long. We put gas on one and lit it and it looked like the Fourth of July. We'd swing them by their tails, and they would get sick, if you know what I mean. My other grandpa taught us that if a snake goes down a hole, pour gas in the hole and stand back. They will come flying out of there like an arrow and fly many yards trying to breathe. Don't get upset, we were just kids, learning. We were always looking for some action and its like that time we found a solid round, hard ball about four inches in diameter. We tried and tried to break it. One day I threw it down on the concrete as hard as I could and my body sort of went forward over it. It came back up and hit me square in the forehead and about knocked me out. Years later I figured out it was a cannon ball. It about killed me just playing around with it trying to break it.

My grandpa had a rocker, soft leather gray with cushioned arms, and I think the footrest popped out. It wasn't as plush as rockers nowadays, but it was simple. One of my brothers cut—sort of sliced—three-inch cuts into the arm of the chair, about three or four lashes. I remember that my grandparents were so very upset. Nobody would admit to have cut it, and everybody was grilled. It was terrible to see the hurt. My grandparents tried to help and love us and we were so disrespectful. Where did it come from? It seemed to be continuous. I never got past the "why." And then to deny it all the way to the grave. I guess what puzzled me was that this all started at such a young age, practically in the mid-sixties. Just a mean gene implanted in the oldest child of five boys. I still don't know for sure who did it, but it was definitely one of those moments that you see the hurt and rejection of an innocent party. In a spiritual way it correlates with the crucifixion, the beating down of a symbol of love. At one point we gave the rabbit business a try and it didn't work out very well because once we got up to about 150 rabbits a disease hit and wiped out most all our rabbits. We never made a dime off our rabbit farm. That was our first business venture. We tried and went around to the grocery store dumpsters to get lettuce and it was a lot of work, I mean a lot of work! My grandpa on my mom's side got us in to the rabbit business. He meant well. Our grandparents were trying to help us kids a lot and we did not recognize it at the time for what it was worth to us. Nothing was handed down to us. Seems to me that the oldest had the red carpet rolled out.

I'm not sure if this is true and if it were true, did it have to do with the out of control lifestyle developed by the oldest one?

After my grandpa on my dad's side died of a heart attack, the vultures moved in and were lowballing my grandma on all the farm equipment and anything that wasn't tied down. One of the stories I remember is my great-aunt's husband bought a cow for a low price and my dad did not like it. The next couple of days, I saw that cow and it had a calf by its side. I knew then not to ever be selfish or not to be greedy. His wife had a bunch of metal tractors and one day we asked if we could play with them and she said no. They were her adopted sons' toys who was in prison for arson. I never forgot those kind of experiences and it was a lesson to me that being tight and selfish gives a lasting impression. I will never forget it. It was like she did not want us around at all, a little strange to us. We felt a tinge of rejection and did not really know how to handle it. We had an idea of why although we still did not understand. This was my Grandmothers sister. It may have been a jealousy thing with grandkids, who knows?

My dad wanted us to hoe the garden and do such things we hated to do. If we were not watched, we would not do it. We'd just as soon be down at the creek swimming or just be out hiking in the woods. I swore if I ever got off that farm, I'd never do farming. I thought there had to be an easier way. We five boys were not cut out for farming, I can guarantee that.

The boys were born in pairs until me, and one day the conversation came up as we were discussing with our parents. It came out that they were done and it appeared that I may not have been intended upon. I think they were hoping for a girl on the fourth child, and they were intending on being done. Regardless of the fourth being a boy, they had a fifth. They were definitely done at that point, although I got the impression I was not meant for. They felt bad that I did not have a brother to pair up with. I think that stemmed from my dad being an only child and my mom being ten or twelve years older than her brother. I grew up somewhat alone and some of it stemmed from the financial demands of my parents having five boys. Not attending preschool or kindergarten made it tough to adjust to a social lifestyle, plus having a dysfunctional family really threw a kink in my social behavior in a big way. Oh, but look what the Lord has done. I can see clearly now.

As I spent time at Grandma's house, I noticed she became a crutch for our family. It was my parents who depended on my grandma to wash us, help us out with food, and probably help us out with things we did not know of back then. One day we were sitting on the back of an old fifty-something pickup truck cutting watermelon under a big shade tree. There was a big knife we used, and one of my brothers threw it, and it stuck in my older brother's leg right above the knee as he sat there. Everybody's eyes got really big as my grandma had to take the knife out and tend to the wound. Back then, it seemed the older generation that was born in the early 1900s had a concoction for anything. We did not go to the doctor every time we got a scratch. Why? I don't know. We were taught to stick it out until the thresh level was high enough to truly set off alarms. I believe it was Joey who got stabbed in the leg at a young age. He turned out okay from the incident, but it is one of those things you never forget. Watermelon, salt, jokes, comfort, and a stabbing? That is strange.

By the time I started walking, I was surrounded by bicycles and wrestling. I came to find out my grandpa from Mom's side was a junker / picker. He kept us in bicycles. We had a dirt track out in the field down off the Olive Branch property. One time there was a collision, and one of us was on the ground, and here came somebody around the fourth turn and ran over his neck. He stopped, and the chain guard was on his neck. He lived but was hurt. We wrecked bikes, rode or stood on seats, no hands, ramps, and all that stuff. We also got a motorized bike, and my grandpa put a seat or board on it so three or four people could get on the bike all at one time. One-time Robby hit a ditch, and my middle brother went up in the air about eight feet and landed back on the seat ten or twenty feet in motion. We called it a picnic table seat. Robby escaped from the police on that scooter. He was getting it down Olive Branch Road. He got away. We just laughed. He was one wild buck. One more story on that motor bike in about 1967 with the picnic table seat. We made a track at our rental home. When my middle brother got on that bike one time, it would not stop. It didn't have brakes, the gas got stuck, and he had to ride around for like thirty minutes and could not figure out how to stop. The gas tank on that thing was huge. He finally got the bright idea to run it up a tree. You should have seen it. That thing went up that tree about eight feet and threw him forward with a leap. It was premeditated chaos. The bike finally stalled. I don't know if he got hurt. I believe he still has a scar from that incident till this day. We had so many stories on that bike I don't know which one was best. Robby running from the state patrol and getting away was probably the funniest because he had it throttled out and was leaning forward for every mile he could get. We knew just standing there watching he would get away, crazy stuff. My grandpa that gave us that scooter, on my mom's side is the one that kept us in bicycles, and he had a fetish about wrestling. He would load us on the back of a big Chevy green truck and drive forty minutes to the Charlotte coliseum to watch pro wrestling. It was amazing to see Jack Brisco, Jerry Brisco, Indian wrestlers, and the Infernos. He would take vanilla wafers and cokes and we would eat them on the back of the truck; it was crazy. We would be out late. One time, I think I got my hand slammed in the door of the truck. Normal stuff happened on these trips. We did it often and it was good. He liked having five grandboys. Now that I think about it, he might have been proud to have taken five "wild" boys to those wrestling matches. It is funny how you look at things when you get older. It was as about as wild as it gets. Controlled chaos is what we call it nowadays.

 The same grandpa took us down to Forty-acre rock and turned us loose. We ran around and explored while nobody watched us on these forty acres. At one point I was sliding down a wet cliff headed for death at a deep drop-off, trying to grab plants, trees, or whatever to hold on to. I was a goner. My middle brother came rushing out of nowhere and grabbed my hand and saved my life, no doubt. We looked down the deep culvert and decided it would have killed me. What a terrible memory to have to overcome. I had not given my life to God yet, so I know he was watching out for me knowing I would. God saved me that day. He used my brother to do it. That was not the last time I about got killed.

My Grandpa taught me how-to knock-on doors and buy stuff cheap from people who needed money and then resale the items for more money than what we paid for them. He was a horse trader if I ever met one. Anybody ever heard of "Pickers?" I loved that. He would come pick me up and we'd ride around in his station wagon and buy junk. He'd resell the junk and trade. I learned this at a young age and now still do it today. It is a hobby. I just do it because I know how to do it. A wild story about him was one Christmas we got a call from him to ask if we wanted to go cut a cedar Christmas tree. We said yes, there were three of us boys at home that day. He came by in an old blue Ford station wagon and picked us up. He took us down to Marshville or somewhere and we just cut down a cedar tree and threw it in the car. We went back through Monroe for some reason and he kept saying he hoped his brakes didn't go out. We were going down highway 74 coming from a place called Hilltop toward a smokestack down a hill and there was a stoplight at the bottom of the hill. I was in the front seat. The light was red and there proceeded an eighteen-wheeler across the intersection and he started pumping the brakes. The brakes did not work, we were going about 50 mph. We were holding on for dear life headed right toward the big rig and we were going to go under it. All of a sudden, he jerked to the left and dodged it like something in the movie Vacation. He whipped it back to the right and kept going like it didn't even happen. He laughed so hard we were laughing at him laughing. He almost killed us. It was really close, no joke. We made it home and got the tree out and he headed back up to Monroe to get his brakes checked out he said. Well, about 12 minutes went by and all of a sudden, our lights went out in the house, the electricity went out completely. We were in the dark and cold in early December with no parents at home. It was hours later we got a call that our grandpa was in the hospital, his brakes went out up at the fork and he could not stop for the stop sign. He hit an electric pole and broke his neck. It was a very strange turn of events. We had a tree and about got killed and now he has broken his neck. A long story short, it wasn't long after that they found cancer and one of the last thing's he did for us was to give us silver dollars on Christmas. It was tough, he did not survive the cancer. He passed away, he didn't say much in passing, he had to have been in deep sadness is my thought. It was unbelievable at the junk he left behind. He was a good grandpa while he lasted. I learned from him and he was funny. Life is short so he was definitely enjoying the ride is all I have to say about that.

Baptist was the denomination that I was born into. We fought and on Sundays struggled with going to church. If our parents did not monitor us at church, the older ones would slip out back and wander the streets for forty-five minutes. The first time I was dropped off in a class, I cried so bad I was in shock. I never had social relations, and I was freaked out. It is actually sad to look back at myself knowing I came out of such a screwed-up family. I didn't even know this was coming. I would use the bathroom on myself and be such an animal because I had no education in social responsibility. All I knew was loneliness and violence. We had very little love in the family. It was strange. I saw some signs of caring and love from my one grandmother, although it was less common and definitely not the majority in our lives. We cannot place uncivil into a civil environment and expect the uncivil to be changed in the twinkling of an eye. I do not understand this method. Civil behavior is a learned behavior over time. Some get chances to grow in to change and some do not.

So, when did I commit to God? It was at the high jump. It was a field day at Wingate Elementary School. All the beautiful people were there. I entered the High jump, broad jump and some other competitions. I was doing well having practiced at home with the crew. It got down to a couple of us, me and a black friend named Earnest. I prayed to God, "If you'll help me over…" He did. I got a ribbon and was so very proud. It's one of those episodic memories that he did his part and I have remembered that day for over fifty years. I practically gave my life that day over something as small as a high jump. God did it for me. I wasn't born a high jumper. That day the Holy Spirit floated me over that bar. I still have my blue ribbon in one of my thirty scrapbooks. God was faithful that day and I have been faithful. Not perfect but faithful. He has been faithful back to me and it has not been perfect at all. I call it sweet redemption, it is great.

There is such thing as Father hunger. It is a yearning for the Father. When our maternal father does not actuate the expectancy then people tend to start asking, who and where is my father? This pertains to some of my reasoning for leaning toward a spiritual father and it became common day reality. It took me forty years to get there although He never gave up on me. Psalm 119 talks of this belief and how that is all we have to do is to sincerely believe and stand on the Word of God, he will prove himself over time. New beginnings was all it took, a Father hunger that helped in starting the search for Redemption. It all started, off a little road called "Olive Branch".

I want to tell a couple of instances of Mother Nature. There is the subject of lightning. I have seen and felt the power of lightning twice. One time I was in a metal building outside trapped in a bad storm, and lightning hit the area so close that it jolted my body. It was a sign to me at the power and strength of Mother Nature. I never forgot the power felt. I felt like I was going to get hit by lightning that day. The other time was the time I was running for my grandma's door, and lightning hit twenty-five feet from me. It was in my sight for sure, a ball of fire that shoots arms of electric fire out to each side. The most unbelievable sight a person could see without getting killed. God occasionally showed his power through mother nature, it was episodic and times that I will never forget. Another incident was when we were in the old 1965 Fairlane Ford driving to Stacks store, and we were almost there. You have to go down a hill, cross the bridge, and go up the hill and there is the store. We were ready to go down the hill when a tornado came down that creek just as pretty as you please and sucked every drop of water and trees up like a giant vacuum. A godly sight to behold. I was learning about God through nature and didn't even know it. And then we all have experiences with rain. In North Carolina in the late 1960's and early 1970's, I remember it being so hot, I would just sit out in the yard and it poured down rain. The rain would beat down and it would tempt you to just want to sit out in it and get drenched. Sometimes I had nothing on but shorts, and it just sort of sticks in my mind like it was strange or something. It was a sense of freedom and, in an odd sense, spiritual. We had a dog, half Saint Bernard and half Pointer that we got from a friend named Eddie. Sebastian would just run with me and play in the rain. Why am I writing this? I guess it was all I had, lonely child with a dog, sort of realized God was over our lives through mother nature. It was a pleasant experience. Even though we thought we were alone, God was always with me. We had great weather in North Carolina. As I said before I have seen the power when I saw lightning pop from thirty feet away as I was reaching for the door to go in. I have been in a metal building with lightning popping so close you could feel its energy. I saw that tornado suck up a creek and clean it out. We had all the other usual weather to where we'd build a gigantic snowman or bike in the sun covered with oils. We never saw floods or fire though. About every thirty or forty years a terrible hurricane may hit the coast but all in all we were nestled up there about two hours from the beach and two hours from the mountains. Not a bad little area in the '60s to run wild and grow. We were free with no rules, although with the way the world was back then, we mostly just hurt ourselves, not too much harm to others. Well, I guess that is not fair to say after reading on.

Along about this same time in history we would occasionally be over at my grandpa's house in Wingate N.C. It was directly on highway 74 between the highway and the railway. The house had a tin roof. Have you ever heard the rain hit a tin roof? Anyway, we boys would go out to the highway in June or July and throw debris in the highway as cars would be headed for Myrtle Beach. I about got hit one day. We would wait on a group of cars and then throw a broom or a board out in the road for a car to run over it. They would hit the debris and keep on going. It sort of reminds me of the house that has a mean dog. When you approach the house you know the dog is going to come chase you. When the cars would approach we would unload all sorts of debris in the middle of Highway 74 for the tourists to run over. Nobody ever told us not to do it. We grew tired of it and moved on to more entertaining pleasures.

We moved around a couple of times in the 1960's. My theory is that my parents thought they could rent the house for more than they could pay rent at another place. I don't know. One house was an old two-story in Wingate built in 1800's with high ceilings, and it was cold in the winter time. I bet we rented that house for nothing. After we moved back to Olive Branch Road, they tore the house down. That old house was across the highway from my mom's parents' house on highway 74. After that stint of time renting, we moved back to Olive Branch Road right up the road and rented from an attorney in town. We stayed there a couple years and then moved back to the original brick home.

Black-and-white TV was commonplace in the 1960s, and we watched Bonanza, and the regulars like Andy and Lucy. We got a color TV in about 1968 or 1969. Hawaii Five-O, and I remember Tom Jones was very popular. We had to watch Lawrence Welk, which was strange, and Ed Sullivan, Hee Haw, and Archie Bunker came on later. The old sitcoms after school were watched as well. We had a pattern developed for years of after-school sitcoms, and I thought that was such a waste. There was so much time wasted away. It was a stagnant time because both parents were not home, and we found ourselves on our own to do whatever we wanted to do with whomever. I am not complaining. It was just odd. The only movies we saw was at a drive-in. I never went to a theater as a young child. One drive-in was good and one was bad, and my dad would park across the street and watch the XXX movies with us in the car. What kind of impression is that on a child? Seeing all that jazz live action as a ten-year-old. It is a form of abuse in my eyes. Put the child out there and let him figure it out. And then there is the magazines lying around the house. It messed me up a little bit, and I had to overcome with God helping me to get through that valley. I do not care for porn and do not want anything to do with that being a part of my life now or when I am gone. It is unhealthy for children and a tough demon to shake. I beat that demon with the help of God.

Along about this time I remember my dad used to take us kids out cruising around the area. This was in the late sixty's era. I remember one time we saw a car coming down the road and it just went to the wrong side of the road and hit another car head on. We just sat there in shock that we would see stuff like this and then move on. Another time we saw a car top a hill on the wrong side of the road and hit another car head on. There was a lot of drunk driving going on in the sixty's obviously. There were a lot of crashes. I am not sure that people used seat belts back then, I don't remember using them. People would live though. Drinking and driving seemed to be pretty normal back in the day where I come from. We had a local race track up in Monroe we occasionally got to go to. It was a dirt track called Starlight Motor Speedway. To us it was big time to get to go see real cars race up close. It was loud and it was action packed. Between races there would be competitions down on the dirt track for children. I vaguely remember this so it must've been in around 1965 or so. Later on in the seventies we occasionally went to the time trials at The Charlotte Motor Speedway, I believe they were free admission, not real sure about that.

About 1965 or so, we'd be at my grandma's house and we played outside most of the time while they were canning and doing kitchen stuff. My brother told me when my grandma would come outside, they wanted me to say a cuss word out loud and watch her reaction, just for meanness. I remember it like I remember a plane flying by at the time. She did come out, and I said a cuss word. I may not have said it loud enough and had to say it again. I hate that I did that. She gave me a look like, "I declare." What in the world? She didn't say much, and everybody thought that was good. Sometimes we'd do something and she'd say, "Go get a switch off the tree." They did burn our butts some, but we'd run most of the time and nobody could catch us. It is sad when I think about some of the horrible things we did to people that had good intentions of helping us, it was really a mean gene.

In about 1968 or so, we snuck out to the barn down at my grandpa's farm, and straw was everywhere. My oldest brother pulled out a pack of cigarettes and lit one up. We all smoked at five or ten years old. Later while we were self-absorbed in other shenanigans, we saw the barn was on fire. Our grandpa lost his tractor, burned his arm really bad, and was hurt badly emotionally. No firetrucks, they had buckets of water. How pitiful that is, grandkids, five boys messing around with idle time. It was awful, and it did not get any better. It was one of the worst things, a terrible fire and all our fault. We never admitted it. They knew who the guilty parties were.

One of my brothers had a favorite cat that was sitting on the back porch one day licking his face and paws. My oldest brother was in his cowboy outfit riding the pony. He had a .22 rifle and said, "You see that cat?" We were like, "Don't shoot him." He shot the cat right in front of us, and the cat died. What kind of sign was that? He used to ride that pony around, and it was a little wild. The pony would raise up, and he would end up breaking the pony. He had a shirt with dangling brown and white fringe that matched the pony. He had the hat too. Where all of that came from, I don't know. It must've been a birthday present or something. I have a picture of him on Princess the pony. Pictures are worth a thousand words and still never tell the whole story.

When we were children, if my oldest brother said to clean, we had to clean or get forced to clean. Did I mention that we tied off ropes around some trees for wrestling? He put on a mask, we had to call him Bolo or he would beat us up? It was all funny and everything but who would have known that it turned out to be real in life and death situations, control issues.

I remember when I started school, I was a nervous wreck. I had not ever been around other people very much and did not know how to act. I had only been at home. I was afraid and scared to say anything. I peed my pants regularly; it would go everywhere. I had a tendency to be so shy that I was afraid to ask if I could go to the restroom. It was a thing to where I was afraid to speak up, no confidence in myself. This mental block and inability created havoc. I was too shy to communicate verbally. I was scared and tormented to think I could express myself verbally. I felt mentally robbed by not going to any kind of school or preschool. I did not even know there was such a thing as kindergarten or preschool. It took me a year and a half until I met Ms. Carlin in the second grade that I started feeling comfortable. I had no social skills. Ms. Carlin kind of took me in as a teacher's pet and helped me fit in. Believe it or not, Ms. Carlin died while I was still young, it was very sad to me and I never said anything about it because I honestly believe nobody would have understood the impact she had on my life. She did understand my issues and helped me big time to overcome the fright and shyness to a high degree.

At our home, we had one of those six-foot-wide stereo cabinets on four legs that the legs were about five inches long. When you open the top lid, there was a huge radio dial, turntable, and probably an eight-track. My parents would put records on, such as Charley Rich, Johnny Cash, Patsy Cline, and Hank Sr. We grew up listening to country. When they weren't there in '68 on, we started Creedence, Beatles, and slowly worked into Led Zeppelin and then we found freedom in Alice Cooper. Rare Earth enters in the late sixties along with smoking pot, doing acid, and drinking mushroom tea. We were living the dream, we lifted weights, got high, and lived life with no central air or heat. Our heat was a kerosene heater that took thirty minutes to get hot. A lot of the time we did not have heat and used the electric stove. Sometimes they'd bring a couple of gallons of kerosene or something if it was going to be really cold. Now that I think of it, I'm not so sure that we weren't just poor.

We used to play army with our neighbors who had five boys as well. One time we built a fort-type jail and tied the second oldest boy that lived next door up in there. About all day we left him there and threw rocks and dirt clods at him from a distance. We left him there till dark. When we would walk around the countryside, we'd often take what weapons we could find. Somebody brought a .22-caliber rifle one day, and as we were down on the creek marching up and down like soldiers, the gun went off and hit the second boy that lived next door in the back of the calf. The doctor said his calf muscle was so big it stopped the bullet from hitting the bone. Later in life I remember sometimes when I would get jeans, I had to split the seam at my calf because the jeans were too tight and it was really uncomfortable on my strong calves. We would be hiking for miles on end all day sometimes and not take water or food. We would drink out of the creek. It was a great thing to be able to take off hiking in the woods as a child and not be on a clock to be home. It was not normal but it gave life a feeling of freedom. All the walking made our leg muscles very strong. Our neighbor that got shot is deceased now.

We were awful. We had nicknames for people and that was not good. I apologize for that. His name was Bill.

We got a new station wagon one time, maybe new, not sure. Anyway, it was new to us. We hadn't had it a day or two when I threw a rock and busted the window out of it. I was throwing a rock at my two brothers and obviously missed them. The funny thing was that my dad came out and was like "who busted out that window"? I told him that "they" did it and he commenced to whip the heck out of both of them. Later, my middle brother was like "how did you convince him that two people threw one rock"? I really don't know the answer to that but they let me have it for a long time over that ordeal. I had to pay them back over time I remember. I am not sure but I think I did bust that window out. For real though, some innocent party took a licking for something they did not do.

It leads me to wonder and I still say somebody pushed my brother next to me off a thirty-foot cliff to a rocky bottom and he had to have his head sewed up. I often wondered if he fully recovered. He landed headfirst on a blue slate rock. I often wondered if somebody pushed him. It messed him up pretty bad. I wonder if it affected his brain any. He seemed to be alienated from the rest of us from that point on. Possible trust issues, I don't know.

My mom saw another man for a while I remember. Let's not call his name here to protect the innocent. She used to get cars and trinkets from him. She would drive a Continental, a Cadillac, Fords. This man had a house close to ours, and my mom took me there a time or two. He gave me a watch one time attempting to butter me up. It was weird beyond reason. Obviously, the community did not know; he was married too. I was old enough to know, probably around 1967. This reminiscing about the past reminds me too of a nanny (African American) who used to watch us. She lived down on the curve going toward Richardson Creek bridge. She must've watched us when we were really young, but I remember an afro american nanny that babysat us. I have very faint memories of that house she lived in. It got torn down later, and the lot is still vacant. This memory is a little vague although I do remember the house they lived in.

SWEET REDEMPTION

We had a lot of school bus stories. One story was about a girl vomiting on the back of my brother. Another was a guy poked my brother with a knife. We'd smoke pot before we got on the bus and stink up the bus. My big dog Sebastian (my grandmother pronounced it "Sebasca"). She could not say "Sebastian". It was hilarious. Sebastian would stop the school bus in the road and bite at the tires. I guess she wanted the kids to stay awhile as they yelled out the windows at her. She loved the attention. She got hit more than once. One time there was broken glass thrown along her running path and her paws got cut up pretty bad. She came home and there was blood all over the back porch. I wrapped her feet up and she did okay. She just would not stop bringing dead animals up to the back porch, almost every morning. My grandmother's dog's name was "Snooky", way before any Hollywood shows came around. Snooky lived to be very old, I mean very old. It was a chihuahua that barked and showed its teeth in a ferocious manner when company showed up. Another one of those school bus stories is that my oldest brother took somebody's basketball and the driver said not to throw it out the window. He threw it out the window, and the driver ran the bus out through a field as they fought. We got the bus out of the field and went on. I don't think anybody mentioned it to the school, but it was remarkable nobody got hurt. The driver was one of the five boys next door.

We rented up the road for a few years, like I said, and my brothers got a hold of the double barrel shotgun my dad had. They were shooting one barrel at a time when it dawned on them that I did not know anything about the shotgun. I was the youngest, so they loaded two shells and pulled both ears back and showed me how to pull both triggers at the same time. It just so happened a squirrel came dancing by, and they said, "Shoot the squirrel with both triggers." I pulled the triggers, and the force was so strong it knocked me backward, and I fell on my rear end, holding the double barrel shotgun. They thought that it was something. They laughed for ten minutes while I recouped. I guess I was a hero. The squirrel lived; I missed, will never forget that incident.

My mom used to get her hair done at a farm out in the country. She would let us go and play outside while she did the hairdresser thing. One day about three of us went with her, and we started throwing rocks at the pigs and hogs. It was fun. My middle brother threw a rock about thirty yards, and it lodged in a pig's ear and stuck. It was an amazing shot. That pig went crazy and started running around charging into other pigs, and we ran. It was the funniest thing you've ever seen. Don't tell the PETA people; we were just kids without supervision. We commenced to climb the silo and got to the top and went in. It was full of corn, and it seems a person could die in a silo of corn. It was so hot up there it was unbelievable. One went in while the other held a hand. You do sink, but we didn't know exactly how far you'd sink, I think those silos are dangerous, boy's need to be watched at all times.

At this rental house we lived at for a couple of years there was one room out in the barn we had a homemade ping pong table in. We would go out and play ping pong and play chicken with different games for hours on end. We were all jumping around and frolicking one day and all of a sudden, a four by four hard pole fell from the top of the building and planted right in the middle of my head. I don't know how it did not kill me. It was bad enough to see stars for a while. We had to shake stuff off like that, back then you just bore the pain unless you were just absolutely dying or needed to be sowed up. I guarantee you I received a mild concussion that day and I have never forgotten it either. So easy to lose your life if you don't watch yourself. That was rare odds that pole would fall dead center on my head.

One of the chicken games we would play out in that building at the rental property we lived at for a while was with darts. We were out there one day and we played darts a lot, we started playing chicken with the darts. We would throw a dart at each other's bare feet. If you moved your foot then you were chicken. Those darts stuck in the floor pretty good. I remember one of my brothers won the game. He let the dart stick in his foot. I will never forget that either. Some of the things we did to win a game of chicken was absolutely crazy. This sort of reminds me of Jarts. I wonder who in their right mind would buy five boys a game of Jarts. We are lucky nobody died from that game. Cornhole is a lot safer but we did not have that in the sixties.

Bow and arrows were a rare sight, and I discovered them in the magazines that came. I ended up getting a cheap one for Christmas one year. I was happy, watching the arrow go up and up and turn and fall to the ground. It was amazing. One time I shot it straight up and lost it in the sky and stood still thinking "I hope that thing doesn't hit me". It took about ten seconds or so and it finally landed. That arrow fell within three inches of my nose. It stuck in my shoe between my big toe and second toe. I had to wear the shoe with a hole in it and I felt bad, somewhat scared for a few days knowing that arrow could have killed me. I was an emotional wreck for a while. I never told anybody that story. I did talk to God quite often about how he saved my life that day. Just another example of how God protected me because he had a plan.

In or about 1969 or so, we had that .22 caliber rifle, and one day, I aimed it up in the air hoping possibly to hit a cow about two or three hundred yards away. I aimed pretty high realizing the bullet would drop. It took a while but soon enough the cow commenced to bucking. I didn't stick around to see if it lived or not, it probably did. It was like when a child is excited to have a bb gun and kills that mockingbird, it gives you a sick feeling if you know what I mean.

Also, in about that same timeframe we heard some kind of a joke about "what about the buffalo?" I don't know if it was on Hee Haw, Laugh in or what but the joke was told over and over again in our home. The story was told so much from my dad that we started calling him "Buff." I was thinking that we must not have had much respect to call our dad such. It leaked out to the grandmothers and others, we just called him "Buff." When I think back on that, there is no doubt we had trouble outside the home and we had trouble inside the home. We did not even realize the degree of dysfunction. I was going through some of my mom's stuff the other day and found a bracelet my dad owned. On it was the word "BUFF". I feel better now, seems if he had a bracelet with his name on it, then it must not have been as disrespectful as I may have thought. I just thought it was disrespectful to call our dad "Buff". It was just "not" normal. That is very strange when I think about it. My mom and everybody called him "Buff."

I remember my oldest brother and I walking around out in the woods one time and we were about a half mile out when we found a cooter, or a big snapping turtle, as it is really called. My brother made me go back to the house and get a knife so he could cut the turtle's head off. So here we go. I ran to the house and got a kitchen knife and ran back just so we could see the turtle bleed to death. That picture still sticks in my mind. I don't know what all the other options were at that point. Surely, we could have just went on about our venture and made it a good adventure. Maybe it should have been a clue to me that the future would hold more of the same. I don't know but that wasn't good. My mind was wondering when I was headed back with the knife as to what degree he may go with that knife. I will admit that thought. It did not end to good for the cooter.

On a hot summer North Carolina day, there were some of us brothers down at the school real early for my oldest brother to practice baseball. Some of my friends were there early as well. My oldest brother caught one of my friends up on the third floor of the school house. My brother hung him out the third-floor window by his ankles. A lot of people witnessed this incident. I could not believe it. I thought that I was getting ready to see a death for sure. He was screaming for dear mercy. My brother finally brought him back in the window and we went through the rest of the day like normal. I don't forget stuff like this. We used to practice petty theft down at the dugout by shoving our arms up the drink machine and wedging a free drink out for a hot summer day. We did stuff like this all the time in our spare time. It is odd but true.

On one of those hot summer days I was with a couple of buddies of mine and we were playing around at a little league game and wandered off. We found ourselves on a landing strip and went on to the hangar where there was a small yellow plane. One of us threw a brick through the window of the plane and then commenced to rip the sides off. We totally destroyed that plane. We went on about our business, the three of us, my two friends and I. Later on, we were picked up and ended up confessing. They said they got our fingerprints, not likely, but still we admitted it. They showed me the jail and took me to visit a juvenile delinquent home. There were some children in there that I saw and it seemed like a strange atmosphere. I received ten years' probation and visits from an officer. This led me to be protected by the police on a different crime later so I would not be sent off to a home. A few years later while still on probation my oldest brother was sitting in jail. He set us up with breaking and entering into the high school, loaning us his car to break in and take whatever. What we did not know was that he was going to narc on us so he could get out of jail. He did say part of the deal was not to arrest me because I would have been sent off to a juvenile delinquent home. My other two brothers were arrested. When my middle brother went to jail, he had to empty his wallet, and out fell two joints. They did not arrest him for that, but they did come get all the stuff out of the barn that we had stolen. How bad is that? I remember being really scared when the police came and picked up the stolen merchandise. I think it is terrible, nothing to brag about, just dysfunctional.

I did go on the shock treatment tour of the home for juvenile delinquents. It did make me realize I needed to stay straight. Looking at this place as an eight-year-old child was a crossroads for sure. That was a good time to make a decision. It seemed to me that I would never make it straight. The odds were stacked against me and I was conscious of this, so I leaned toward myself and God because I was scared to trust anybody. God pulled me through. I hit a couple of bumps at sixteen and eighteen and so forth, but I never did get caught doing any major crime. Driving drunk may have been my biggest offenses. I had the fun and never outright paid any price. I paid the price God's way through ups and downs in life, but he knew I would be better for it. I trusted and talked to God. I never heard that voice, but I had the faith and depended on him to direct me. He did. I totally give all credit to him for being faithful over time. When a child looks up to the sky, they know there is a God over all this creation. A child born in Africa, Mongolia, or the Arctic Circle, they know. When a child looks up, they know there is a God over all creation. I know this because it happened to me. I often sat staring into the sky, thinking, "God, I was born here, but where are you taking me?" I don't know how many times I sat and truly believed that he would take care of me if I would just keep acknowledging him and try to make the best and right decisions day to day that would make the world a better place. I had to make myself a better person first and that is when I needed his direction and help. My point here is that people know. When we are born into the "not so pleasant." God knows it. He wants us to believe so he can prove himself. I stuck to my belief and he brought me out. It did not happen overnight. I did not go from a messed-up person to an angel overnight. Again this is the Father hunger.

On a different note, one time I did something mean to my middle brother and took off running. Right when he was going to catch me, I crouched so he would trip over me. His knee hit where my kidneys are, and a couple of hours later, I was in an ambulance headed for the hospital. I could not believe the pain. I had back pain for years, and God healed my back later. I remember it was at Lake Lure, we broke into a pool at the hotel at like one in the morning and I was swimming and my back popped really funny and my back was like healed. I couldn't believe it. One time I ran into the forehead of the brother next to me with my nose playing football. Blood went everywhere, I broke my nose in three places and had to have surgery. I ended up in the hospital a couple of days for that. Another time my middle brother and I were throwing darts at a wasp on the ground, and as we were looking closely at the damage to the wasp, as I bent over to get the dart, the wasp got on my finger. I came up with the dart suddenly and jabbed my brother in the eye. It has affected him ever since. I felt bad, he was already color blind and now I about jabbed his eye out. We were lucky it missed by a few centimeters. It could have put his eye out permanently.

This one girl I grew close to in elementary school was a special tomboy friend of mine. She used more of the brain than me, but she had that drive I have. I channeled my drive toward mischief, and she channeled her drive toward music. In my life I have always been like a turtle, looking, moving slow, but when I arrive, I arrive fully loaded and prepared for anything. I noticed this in my old friendship with my old friend. She had direction, guidance. We both ended up being successful people and hooked back up through the Internet. Interesting that God helped me to cross that finish line with having my life together after all the discombobulated issues in my life as a child. God protected me and gave me enough wisdom and a good wife to help me to be here writing this today. It is a wild and crazy journey, but he brought me through. I turned out okay and somewhat successful. Jayne passed away in her sleep as of this writing in 2019. I sent flowers from Kentucky and am grateful I had mailed her a book earlier that year called "The uncommon woman". I loved Jayne so very much, a distant dear friend. It was very sad to me that she died so young and suddenly. That is why sometimes I like to give gifts now, why wait? You never know when someone may pass on into eternity. No better time than now to love one another and show it.

Needless to say, being in an uncontrolled environment, we were pretty much on our own to control our emotions. I would find myself occupying my time with cleaning the house up and placing everything in order. It was usually a messy house. I found that I liked to organize and clean, clutter was not something I enjoyed living it. Even though I tried to occupy my mind I still fell short. Occasionally each one of us would be pushed to our limitation. One time I got so mad at my brother I threw a steak knife at him as hard as I could, sitting at the dinner table. Now that is drawing the line. At a young age and self-control maxed out, I was pushed to my limit. I hate that I did that, although God looked out for me. My dad slapped me across the mouth and his class ring hit my lip and my lip swelled up like a croissant. It was bad. I did what I did, and it was bad, as far as the outcome of it. All of it was over an argument and name-calling. I am sure it goes on today in schools and places. What was different was it was a family issue, and again, God intervenes in all situations and protects us who believe. I mean I could have gone back to jail if it had been a true assault to where somebody was stabbed.

We'd hear our parents and grandparents talk of stories and tales stretched to no end. One story was that there was a cop in the local community that got caught messing around with a girl and the people who caught him nailed his testicles to the floor until police showed up. Now here we are as kids and hearing stories like this, it was just out there and I will never forget it. Now the good thing is that I quickly learned that older people know stories. I started asking questions of my elders when I got older because they knew some of the history such as my grandma on my dad's side told of hangings on Richardson Creek and how their necks would stretch out a foot or two after the neck broke. Some of the local community watched. This must have been in or around 1915, not real sure if she witnessed the hangings or if the stories were just being passed down the generations.

There was a back way to bypass the main road to head up to Charlotte; we took it often. One day I noticed a black mark on the white car. I didn't think too much about it. One day I was riding with my mom and I noticed a lot of people just all around the road and it seemed dangerous. My mom told me she had just hit and killed a black boy recently, and she would drive through there really quick. We did not have cellphones back then, so I have no idea how that went down but it was like it didn't happen but it did. Amazing, today is a lot different if somebody got killed it practically makes metro news. It was like no big deal and my family wasn't nice when it came to discrimination. My family was discriminate but never talked of being in a clan. I am still stunned at some of the prejudice that was in among our side of life, I got past it, although I never forgot it. I have other stories where we were attempting to keep it between the tracks of nondiscrimination and some are quite embarrassing, I have to say.

Dave Gardner was a comedian back in the '60s, and my mom and dad would put on the old comedy record and we'd sit around and laugh. I guess that was good. It was clean, we did have Stegall reunions where a bunch of people get together and ate the food dishes they brought. They'd sit around and talk about father's fathers. It was cool to see all these old folks. Then you'd hear about so and so died. It is a repeating cycle and eventually it will rotate to all. I guess I got that out of all those family reunions. Now we are older and past fifty. Young people say that we are old now. The sixties were filled with a lot of fun and it was the influx of the flower power generation. We were rolling into the seventies full steam ahead and what a transitional time in history we were in for. The early seventies were the best times as far as music and good times.

1970's

I was sixteen when my dad died. This must've been around 1978 is a guess. Diabetes got the best of him. Once he was going to lose his leg, he pretty much took himself out with pills and drinking wine. The doctor told him to quit drinking. He made out some bills the night before, called his mother, and went to sleep. I remember specifically him making out those bills, and I wonder what they were—medical and life insurance would be a guess. Anyway, he was being nice that night, and I knew something was not right. The next morning, my mom was there, and she said his body was hard, and she called the ambulance to come get the corpse. I think they dropped him. I heard a big noise back there. We did not do an autopsy because we pretty much had an idea since a lot of the valium and other pills were missing that we sneaked.

Some of the many stories about my dad are like when I was fourteen or so out running drunk with a friend, I passed the whorehouses and saw my dad being hauled out on a stretcher. We kept going and ended up in Charlotte. I ended up with the VW and lost my friend somewhere along the way. I wrecked it and hooked back up with him the next day. We didn't care. I think my dad had a heart attack at the whorehouse. That was what I heard. I mean it really was not a topic to bring up like that "we saw you at the whorehouse Buff, what happened"? There is something wrong with that.

One of the sickest things was the Dachshund dog he owned was chewing a hole in his underwear after he pooped while he was passed out on the bed. The dog was chewing the underwear while my dad still had them on. This kind of stuff is hard to make up. I never have liked Dachshund dogs ever since that traumatic sight. Thank goodness, we did not have to rub his back that day. It was this kind of stuff that led to my middle brother pacing the back porch with a .22-caliber rifle swearing he was going to kill somebody. He was on the back porch marching around with a .22 one day. He was going to kill my dad. I think it was bad. He finally was confronted and ended up running away and going to Myrtle Beach. He hitchhiked. He ended up in jail for stealing out of cars and trying to survive. When I saw my brother, I was like "what the heck?". He was definitely roughing it. He was definitely abused as a child. My dad used to make him and us rub his back. As he would go to sleep, we would sneak out of the only air-conditioned room. He would lay back there and yell a victim's name to come "rub my back." One time he yelled for a jar of water, and my middle brother was taking it to him, stopped in the living room, fell to his knees, and proceeded to pee in it right in front of everybody, crazy stuff, oh my gosh.

    This is not really slamming my dad. It was just the way it was in the seventies growing up. This is better than The Seventies Show. I remember when I needed a ride to football practice I was ashamed for my dad to drop me off or pick me up because he would blow snot out the window in front of anybody. It was disgusting and I realized one day that those stains on the side of the car were puke stains. I washed them off more than one time because I wonder if people could figure out that pattern of stains down the side of the car. I mean it was like a swoop of vomit from the driver's door on out toward the rear spreading out as it blew out to the wind, help me Lord. It took some nerve but I had to inconspicuously ask my dad to just sort of drop me off out at the road and he'd be like, "no, I can take you up closer to the gate". I would be like "okay, thank you". That is pitiful but it is what it is. I love my dad. It was a little bit different though growing up in this environment. I don't have too much room to talk. At the time I was selling pot daily. One day we were at gym and somebody in the boy's locker room said that twenty dollars had been stolen out of their gym bag. The coach decided he was going to strip search each individual as they exited the locker room. There was one problem though, I had an ounce of pot in my duffel bag. It got down to the last few boys and I told my friend in crime to go through and get searched, come around to the window and I would hand him my pot. He did, the other kids were watching while I pulled out this bag of pot, wrapped in a gym cloth and handed it through the window. The kids were like "what is that?" We got away with it but they were on our case the rest of the day because somebody told on us, rightfully so. The only other time we about got busted for pot at school was when the middle grade principal took about a dime bag of pot from us and he never called the cops or anything. I can't remember if we got it back when we jumped him or if he kept it. I know we got suspended, I remember that because I would ride the bus to school and walk around the big city of Marshville N.C. all day and get back on the bus to go home. I got caught though because we had to have a parent to sign us back in at the end of the suspension. What a mess it was. I have a lot of room to talk.

    We all experimented with drugs and such. I would take things and experiment with how it affected my mental and physical being. We were looking for that feel good moment when we could get our hand's on stimulant's. Sometimes I would take too much and one day I woke up on my grandma's couch completely naked. It was the couch that my great grandma had died on come to think of it. It was embarrassing because I had to have walked there naked. I remember waking up wondering where I was. When I realized where I was, I was like "I am naked". Then I had to play it off like I must've had a bad dream and I shrouded myself with the throw that was on the couch, had to face my grandmother and slowly headed back up toward the house. This is one of those moments when you just want to get away really quick. I saw firsthand the principalities of warfare and darkness. It was a dark and strange time experimenting with things. I know the difference between good and bad. I know the devil roams around looking for a chance to come against good. I know who wins though. Even though, we have setbacks, we know it is worth it to do good. We make this earth a better place. We are the salt. This may be a good place to emphasize that this book is not a complaint session. This book is written to let people know that a person can get past the problems and issues they might have had as a child. A person can use the winds and storms of life to rise above the issues pecking at them. I learned in ministry that if speaking, speak about the devil for two minutes, and God for twenty-eight minutes. In this writing, it will be a smorgasbord of issues and stories, although the main point, again, is that a person can overcome and get past hard issues. I got past all this stuff and have a clear mind, thank God. The Holy Spirit leads me, and I laugh at bad thoughts and carry on as a successful clear-minded person who overcame, it is redemption, a true, sweet promise.

So, back to some of those crazy stories. Several times as children we were left with the responsibility of hoeing the garden. We had to get all the weeds out. All it took was for somebody to say, "Yawl want to go jump in the lake?" Over time, Richardson Creek became Lake Twitty. We did not have anybody to stop us from going. "Boys, lake?" We dropped the hoes and took off. There was a canoe tied off at a friend of ours house. I think it was Tom's. We stole it quite often and took off. One-time my middle brother dove out of the canoe into the lake head first not knowing the water was only four feet deep. He stopped immediately with his legs looking like the Easter bunny's ears. One time we flipped it, and somebody lost their watch. One time somebody tried to land in the canoe off the rope and straddled it and flipped. We got caught numerous times by the warden, never got wrote up though. There were so many stories behind the infamous canoe. When we would canoe around the new lake over to the other side, we'd walk about a mile to the store whether we had money or not. We did our share of stealing, but this particular store must've had the Holy Spirit over it or something. I don't remember stealing from Mr. Helm's store. We'd have a little bit of change sometimes, and somebody might get a soda. We'd walk back to the canoe and paddle back toward home, observing the beauty, snakes and wildlife. One time we sought how many snakes we could catch and put in the boat; that did not go over very well. Before the dam was built, it was Richardson Creek. We used to go to the creek and swim and explore the woods. We heard a bobcat down there one time, and that was scary. When the dam was built, my oldest brother pushed one of my neighbors off the dam into the water side. We thought he was a goner; he lived and I will never forget that. The water was a scary thing; the other side was even scarier. It was concrete. We were doing something every day that was borderline risky. One time I jumped out of the canoe, and it was over my head. I was just learning to swim and panicked and I almost drowned. My brother grabbed my hand and pulled me up. At least they recognized it and actually saved my life (again) as I remember. At this point in my life I started to realize that God was watching over me. I would often sit on the back steps at home and think. One day I was sitting there thinking about the direction the people in my family had taken, and none of the directions looked too entertaining, mostly jail, prison, alcohol, smoking, sex, drugs, murder, rape, kidnapping, and abuse. I mean, come on. How low can you go? I did the talk and promised God that if he would give me some kind of prosperity and direction, I would give my life and serve him. It did not happen overnight, but when I was tempted, I knew my conscience became real and it was apparent that God was in my heart. Back on those steps in the early '70s, I actually accepted God in my heart again as my Lord and Savior. Again, this reflects on the scripture Psalm 119 in a big way.

Along about this time in 1969 and 1970, the town of Pageland S.C. sold beer to people at sixteen. I know people were driving at sixteen, so when my parents would go to sleep at night, we'd steal the '70 Mach 1 Mustang and run around the country roads. I am pretty sure we were going to Pageland a time or two. That car would fly, three speed on the floor. We also had to get up to help run a paper route. We'd drive from two thirty to five and then go to school. That is where I learned to love the smell of skunk in the early morning air with windows down, listening to "bye bye Ms. American pie". We also had to knock on doors to collect money. I remember seeing a colt born at the Traywick's pasture down on Olive Branch as the sun arose, new beginnings so to speak. This was Randy Travis's house. We grew up with them a little bit after middle school, lot of skipping school and pot smoking going on there in Randy's brothers Cutlass. We had some great times. The Traywick's grew up right down the road about twenty miles from us, and when busing started, we merged together down at the middle school in Marshville, North Carolina. We skipped school, smoked cigarettes, drank, partied, smoked pot and did all these things as boys do. We had affairs and good times. Randy ran some turkey houses and dropped out of school early. He played the guitar; they had a large family. There was a younger brother and a sister my age. Randy won the county fair a couple of times with his talent and eventually went up to Country City USA in Charlotte N.C. His manager was scouting around and picked Randy up, he ended up down in Music City U.S.A. hustling catfish and doing maintenance. He played on stage and eventually got a record deal. He changed his name to Travis. I can't tell all what we did but there were some crimes committed. He never got all that wildness out but now after the stroke I think he has changed. The Lord works in mysterious ways for sure.

Everybody seems to remember when busing students started. When busing started and we had to go to a middle school, I remember my second oldest brother coming home one day and said there was this one teacher that made you hold your hands out and he would smack you on the backside of your hands with a leather strap. This was way beyond getting a paddling, which hurt. I was always scared I would get that teacher. What do you know, when I went into the eighth grade, who do you think my homeroom teacher was? I put it on my bucket list to steal that strap. One day after many escalated events, suspensions, them taking our pot and other issues I just decided to take the strap. I did, I took it and kept it for a long time. I know I was wrong but it was a feeling of revenge I guess you could say. I was probably twelve or thirteen, but to whip someone's hands with a strap? Who would think this was even legal.? After a few more hard paddling's I started thinking, maybe the strap would have been less severe, those were some hard paddling's for sure. We had some wild times in middle school. I remember getting paddled in school a lot. The teacher would take you right outside the classroom door and say "bend over". The Elementary School had twenty-foot high ceilings and was built after the War. The halls were really long like thirty or forty yards long. When that paddle hit, it would be like "POW!" with an echo. Then we had to proceed back into the classroom and most students would glare and the teacher would give a Barney Fife look like "yep, that's what happens when you step on the teacher's toes". Sometimes the teacher would even say something like we don't tolerate misbehavior. The students really wanted to see if any pain was evident. Of course, it did not hurt, yeah right. Some students seemed to be in shock from the trauma. Others were like "did it hurt?' The other thing was, if you had to stand in the hall for misbehavior, there was a chance you may get caught by the hall monitor. If you got caught it was an automatic paddling by the Principal in his office. It was funny because the class did not ever know if you were still out there or not. It may be ten or fifteen minutes depending on the misbehavior. It may end up all good or it may end up like "POW!" with the echo in the hallway. It always hurt although I had to grin and sometimes have enough gall to say "that didn't hurt". It was quite comical now that I look back. One of the worst things in middle school was when the teacher went to make copies one time. I lit a pom-pom with a lighter that was hanging out the air conditioning vent. The air was blowing and when I lit it, the pom-pom lit up like a Christmas tree. I got it put out thank goodness but the smell was really bad and the smoke. It was like, we all knew the teacher was going to show up any second. I was busted. I had to write a paragraph a hundred times. I had help and the teacher flunked me because I had help, it wasn't like he could not tell the other hand writing was not mine. Another time a ceramic bowl fell out of my pocket and busted on the floor in the classroom. When a ceramic bowl breaks on the floor, that is one thing. The smell of the ceramic bowl was another, that was a quick trip to the bathroom to flush evidence. We cleaned it up and made the mistake of putting it in the trash can at the teacher's desk. That did not go over very well. She did not like the smell of marijuana in her face. I don't remember exactly what happened in the end. I ended up graduating high school somehow.

Three interesting subjects come to mind thinking back on these times. Love, giving and visitation at funerals are some subjects that we were sort of on our own with, like having to figure things out on our own. The first one is love. We only saw love through my grandma on my dad's side, and that was through giving. My grandpa on my mom's side gave us toys and such, but we never really learned much about how to love and what love was. I never said "I love you" as a child that I can remember. It was strange and warped. I remember when this one girl kept saying I love you and I would not say it back. It got to a point to where I was called out on it. It took some getting used to or as my grandson might say "I was getting the hang of it". Once I learned the foreign language, I wore it out. I said "I love you every time I went out of the room. I found balance after a while. Giving? Forget about it. We were out for anything we could get our hands on, and I know that is part of why we had such a reputation in the community and with the police. It was true; we were not the greatest people. On the subject matter of funerals by the way, visitation is a subject I learned about. There was a girl that came to the visitation of my brother, and I never forgot it. I know the importance of visitation because of this; people remember. Also, the Bible says to go to funerals and be aware of death. I try hard to practice these traditions.

There was a time in the late sixties and early seventies that I went through some major growing pains in my legs. The pain was on a level of about seven or eight and I never spoke about it much. I dealt with it with God and had an idea that it would go away one day. Some would likely chalk it up as growing pains for sure. It was so bad and really could not do anything about it. I had an idea that the pain was from all the walking we used to do and building of the leg muscles. This went on for a good two years when I was ten or eleven years old. Its just one of those things that while it was going on it leaves you puzzled, will it end? I kept telling myself it would and it finally did end but man, the physical growing pains are real folks, speaking from experience.

In the early 1970's or somewhere in there, we rented for a while like I said and at the rental house up on Olive Branch Road, we had an old barn on the property. It was haunting to be out there and one day it was late and a couple of us were out in the barn. We heard this ghost sound going like "woo ohh woo" for like fifteen seconds and then it would take a break and then do it again. We didn't know for sure but it was really scary. Growing up with all the boys you just never knew what may happen next. We never did find out if it was really a ghost or not, it just went unmentioned, scary stuff. This sort of reminds me of the shotgun again. About three of us were up at the top of the hill about a hundred yards from the house, we were in the road with the shotgun. My middle brother was push mowing the front yard down the hill a little bit. He only had on some short cutoff jeans. He was just a getting it. Somebody said, "Shoot down that way and see if any of the pellets hit him" He was allergic to wasps and when we pulled the trigger, the pellets hit him and he thought he was being stung. He was jumping and dancing around that yard like he was on fire. Every time I think about that, I snicker out loud. I asked him about that not too long ago and he did not know it was gun shot. A lot of stuff went unsaid. In 1971, my oldest brother used to take me out drinking a lot when I was about nine or ten. I would drink chug-a-lug. It didn't take but about one and a half and I would be intoxicated. One afternoon, we stopped into Pizza Hut and I was feeling bad. I mean "real" bad. Drinking on an empty stomach at about twelve years old is not a wise decision. We had a group of five or six. There was an empty glass sitting in front of me. I will be honest here, while people were eating and having a great time, I filled the glass up with vomit. It ran over on the table and some of our group ran out and left me there with one other person. I don't really remember how that turned out but it was an episodic memory for sure, not a good upbringing. In 1971, my middle brother was wild as a buck and at that rental house we had right up the road one time we had a set of clackers. Some won't know what clackers are so go ahead and google it. Anyway, one of us would lay on our stomach on the ground and another person would raise and lower the clackers over the sides of the back at the rib cage area. It would tickle like no tomorrow. The object of the game was to take the torture as long as you could and then say "stop," pretty strange game huh? My middle brother had to be a hero and he did really well on his turn, so well taking the pain that he jumped up and grabbed the clackers and threw them up in the air as hard and far as he could during a feel-good moment. The clackers were spiraling and came down and landed on the electric line. It was that quick. That party ended and we went to find something else to get into. Spontaneous incidents happened all the time and they were so funny. In 1971, we were listening to Led Zeppelin one time, it was the song D'yer maker. My middle brother had his favorite hairbrush he used and was playing around with it. When Robert Plant got into it as we all know he could, my brother sort of took his pleasure and excitement out on the hairbrush twisting it. He broke it in half during the feel-good moment and it wasn't some great feat, it was just the uncontrolled potential we all had and did not know what to do with it in an odd way if that makes sense. This is the kind of stuff we did all the time and it was one thing after another. Pretty funny as I look back at some of the ridiculous stuff we did.

In the early 1970's, my oldest brother would wait on me to get home from school. He loved to wrestle and put holds on me. It was brutal and borderline abusive but man did it ever toughen me up. It made me strong and helped my stamina. He had full control of me most of the time but occasionally I would muster up enough courage to try to take him down. I never fully won, it gave me unbelievably strength and vigor to keep fighting. I don't know if it is fitting to say thank you for the abuse, but it sure made me a stronger person physically and developed a tolerance for pain. Getting up for school was just as bad. I was pulled to floor from the top bunk more than one time as my wake-up call. I did not have a Big Ben.

We use to have this red and white Cadillac back in the day, pretty sharp. At the time I always wondered, how do we keep getting the big cars? It was very strange. This Cadillac had like a five-hundred-cubit block, a four door with a vinyl top. The oldest one used to take it and we would go sometimes. It certainly caused me to lose a couple of hours sleep. He would take it up to the Roses Department Store parking lot and park up at the top of the lot facing away from the store. He would mash the gas to the floor while his foot was on the brake, in reverse gear. Then he would let off the brake suddenly and the car would spin out of control like madness all the way down the hill toward the store doing loops, smoking and doing everything except turning it upside down burning rubber. It was the darndest sight you ever saw. I don't know how it did not flip. It was like the winner of a NASCAR race when they do the burnout. We all just laughed and we would occasionally get in the shopping cart's and ride them down the hill until they either crashed or came to a halt, if you were lucky. That Cadillac though, if certain people knew he was doing that, I don't know if he would have been allowed to drive that car anymore. One time they bought him a hot rod station wagon in the late sixties. That did not last very long, I think it was right before one of his sentences, go figure. He was actually lucky he lived up to the late eighties, no joke.

Domestic violence was pretty routine in our lives throughout. Even when we were babies, my parents fought about sex and alcohol. When we boys became older, around thirteen, we started thinking nobody could stop us. We fought so much. One time my oldest brother was fighting my dad, and my mom threw a two-inch-thick ashtray and hit my brother in the head. The ashtray broke into two pieces. I still have that ashtray. We saw blood at an early age from domestic violence. It was quite disturbing, and on Sunday we'd try to make it to church, not exactly like a normal functioning family. I guess that was what church was for, for sick people. I was quiet as a child and often reflected on our disarray.

I hung around my oldest brother quite a bit when he was out of prison because we got along really well even considering his schizophrenia. I love the guy even though he was as crazy as they come. He would tell me that if the cops stop us, he wanted me to take the drugs and run while he distracted them by fighting them. He always said, "Run as fast as you can and hide, get away, and I will get out later and hook back up with you." He was the type that would be going down the road in his Corvair and just hit a stop sign and break it off for being funny. He would drive on the wrong side of the road and make people play chicken; he always won that game. We would throw rocks at cars, and I saw cars wreck and we'd run. He'd play chicken with trains. A friend got hit by a train with him, and I had heard that it was likely a chicken game. The friend lived but was wheelchair bound. What a prize, huh? He was the Chicken King!

We boys worked at Judd's Restaurant as we grew through our early teens; we bussed tables. It was a family-owned small business who served great food and had that nice smell, the smell of homemade cooking. We would work from three to eleven on weekends and get paid about $8. All of us worked there over the years. After about 1974 or so, Mr. Judd was on his normal routine of taking the money home in a cigar box and he always had a gun. Two people jumped him at his front door and tried to take his money. They shot and killed him. To this day I still believe my oldest brother and a friend of his had something to do with it, there was some strange talk around the house during that great loss. It was quite obvious that most all employees knew the details like we did as far as how Mr. Judd took the money home. That has haunted me to this day that the criminal justice system could not prove that case. I believe this is one reason my brother kept going down the path of crime. I believe he thought he got away with it and was above the law. It may not be the case, just an opinion only. I might be wrong about that murder; I believe nobody ever got punished for the crime through the justice system.

One day I came home, and in the back of the house was a girl in the bed. She seemed to be frightened and did not say anything when I looked at her. I asked my brothers who she was, and nobody seemed to really know. She needed a ride and ended up in our house. Is this kidnapping? I saw two or three kidnapping cases as a child, one to Florida, one from a department store. It made me think that if I saw three or four, how many were there? I just don't believe those were the only ones. There was some kind of control pattern my brother had in his mind, and if he didn't get his way, he wanted to do something in retaliation. This was not normal. Did I mention rape? Girls became a weekly thing in my brother's life at about sixteen and seventeen years old. I went with him one night when he picked up an African American girl and we took her to the dam and went under the chain to get in. He practically threw her on the ground after drinking and doing whatever else that was in the air. He practically made love to her right there on the ground and then asked me if I wanted to get on her. I chose not to because I was a bit flustered and a bit new to this technique of having sex with strangers. We dropped her off in a local hood and went on to our next venture of drinking and getting high. I must've been eleven or twelve. There were other incidents like this although I am not going to expound on them.

We spent a lot of Sundays visiting many different prisons over the years of growing up. I guess prison visits started in 1973 and

1974, not really sure, but that puts me at twelve or thirteen. It was educational, the doors slamming, the noises, the story of fights, smuggling stuff, conversations to be hush-hush, just so much to take in. I had hair to my shoulders, and there was a lot of gay activities among inmates too. I don't like to be around that stuff now, have done a couple of prison visits in ministry, but it is not my calling. I know God said to visit prisons and I may struggle with this a bit because of the shock and awe from experience with prisons as a child. We visited probably twenty prisons or more growing up. My wife watches lockup shows now, and I at first found it hard to watch them, because of the influx of prison life as a child and all the stories that came with it. I was pretty much sick of that lifestyle. It helped me to stay right with God, and I subconsciously knew not to do things that would end me up there. It was hard though because I was raised in a lifestyle riddled with crime and deception. I only ended up in jail a few times, and God helped me to keep it between the lines. He knew I would choose him, and that is why my life did not end up in ruin. It is truly amazing that God would save me to do good. It is what happened, and I know my purpose. All things are possible with God.

Two stories that run close together are related to drugs. One night my second oldest brother came home from the country. I think Pageland. He woke everybody up and swore up and down he saw a UFO. It was big news. After we figured out, he was on acid or PCP and calmed him down, he finally went to sleep. The next morning, he kept saying it landed and burned a spot in the ground. We had to go look for a burnt spot in the ground that day. I was thinking, "Man! We're looking for a burnt spot from a UFO. How crazy?" The other one is that one day we were riding around (this isn't drug related), and a couple of us started wrestling in the car. We stopped the car and took it to the woods. The next day we realized we wrestled in a patch of poison ivy. We had to go get shots and miss school; it was so bad. It was really bad. One day we all drank mushroom tea, and my middle brother pooped right out the back door of the mobile home. Later that night a couple of them started wrestling on the grass and wallowed in that mess and did not know it until they were in the car to get some more beer while tripping on mushroom tea. The smell was enough to make them throw up. But it was one for the books. He drove a Monaco car. That trailer had some awful stories between alcohol, drugs, and sex. We always had good music albums though. Anybody ever heard of Robin Trower? It was a home away from home. There was a little underage drinking going on there, among other things underage.

One time my oldest brother got his picture in the newspaper streaking down the street in Monroe, North Carolina. We got the paper and sort of bragged about it on Sunday. My mom sort of grinned and didn't do anything about it. I guess now that I am older, I sense that not doing something is sort of condoning it. We never did let it out to too many people that it was one of us in the paper. I think we all ran around naked at some time during the streak years, guilty!

Another subject is when my oldest brother rented a trailer in Matthews and worked at PCA. There was a girl he lived with, and I think we all jumped in the bed with her. She was twenty-eight. I am quite sure she was over twice my age at the time. In today's society, she would be put in jail, no big deal back then. On the subject of insurance on vehicles, we sat a VW on the railroad tracks and turned up Bob Seger in the eight-track player. After the train pushed the VW on the tracks a half mile or so, Bob Seger was still playing, talk about "ol time rock 'n roll?". The VW was covered under insurance, so it brought in money. There was a time when cars would disappear and insurance would pay out. There was a time in the late '60s when a military train procession came through Wingate and we should have been saluting. One of my brothers threw a Cherry bomb smoke bomb on the train, and the train came to a halt. We ran like wildfire and never got caught. Eventually the train moved on slowly to the next town. It was a big deal that the train was coming through. I do not remember exactly why it was so important. My brother had to make an episode out of this historical event. I do not miss all these instances. All of these stories and nonsense lead to dead ends. I find it much more appeasing to live a life of abundance and prosperity, doing things that are good.

SWEET REDEMPTION

I went through a stage in life where it seemed there were opportunities to commit fraud in 1976. I hate to admit it, social security paid me because I lost my dad later on and I was supposed to go to college. They kept their end of the bargain but I didn't. I forged signatures on different checks I could find and attempted to push the envelope and it really was not worth the trouble to be honest. I figured out it is better to work for an honest dollar. The SBI tracked me down in Food Lion one day and hemmed me in. I had to commit to paying some money back. Seems like they tried to ID me once or twice, and I never would admit who I was. Temptation can get the best of a person especially with money. The key to it is to change your evil ways, pull out of it, and stay right. I got past the fraud issues that went on for a couple of years. Social Security let me off without paying the money back due to a hardship letter I had help in writing. I had a little bit of a hard time breaking away from fraud. I did though, slowly.

We spent a lot of time around the railroad tracks out behind my grandfather's house in Wingate N.C. We used to place pennies on the railroad track and watch the train mash them beyond recognition. It would make a penny almost as big as a silver dollar. We would climb in between the stopped trains and hang around the tracks a lot. One story that I am embarrassed to tell is about when we had a black friend with us and we were walking down the tracks just living our lives. We spotted another group of people heading our way on the tracks, it was obvious we were going to meet. We were talking among ourselves and thinking it could be a little clash of the titans. Totally out of fear and embarrassing myself I said out loud "it looks like a bunch of black people" except I did not use the words "black people". About that time, I realized we had one of our black friends with us. There was no need to apologize. It was just the way we were raised and I feel bad about it. We recognize things for the way they are and move on past them eventually. Some would say "this too shall pass". He saw first hand how us white people talk when left alone or in this case they may think they are alone. We were awful kids and had that discriminate gene in us to a degree. We loved our black friends although we had the upbringing to be discriminate subconsciously. That was one time I was torn between my true heart and a discriminate upbringing. It was just one of those moments where you can't undo what just happened, not good.

My oldest brother is deceased although I have all his certifications showing he had perfect attendance every year up until like the ninth grade. Off to jail a person goes. What a devastating impact on so many facets of life. The perfect attendance, sports, families, expense, morale, and social well-being. What a devastating blow not only to the family but to the community. It was the start of a terrible run for the next twenty years until he was shot. There is a show called turning point. When all this started, it was a turning point, and no, he did not walk the stage for graduation. It was more about the Beatles, pot, and sexual perversion and taking advantage of people who would not expect such rash behaviors.

We grew up on music, from Hank Senior to Credence Clearwater, Beatles, and Alice Cooper belting out licks at six thirty in the morning before school. We jumped fences to get in concerts with no tickets and were just outright out of control. We had country and comedy too. We went to concerts; we had no money to get in. Even up till the 1990s, I still went to concerts. One top Christian band in the 1990s in their beginnings was Johnny Q Public, they were great. Music is still part of my life of course, although I rarely go to concerts. I like remembering bands as they were in the 1970's. Fleetwood Mac live and Boston were the best sounding bands in the 1970s. We rolled a foot-long joint at a Boston concert and when we pulled it out and lit it, everybody just got high. A Cheech and Chong moment for sure, it was so funny everybody just loved it, good times. Tom Scholz got hurt when he fell and they replayed "Don't Look Back" because he missed some licks. It was one of the best. I thank God for all he has allowed me to see and that I turned out sane. I learned how to grow pot in my spare time, learned about the male and female plants and how to make them bud. I would plant them on the edge of the fields, and when I would hear the combines cutting, I would cut them down. I grew them in other places too. I dried the leaves in the old purple VW that sat out back. You know how hot it would get in that North Carolina heat, especially with the windows up. The smell in that VW was so strong I would just sit in it and wonder if that would make me high. It didn't, but I love the smell of drying pot plants. I never sold my own. I grew it to smoke. I would say I never inhaled, but like Bill Clinton, I would be a liar. That is poor. I smoked pot for twenty years and understand the medicinal purposes for it and agree. I don't desire it, although I do condone it if it is legally prescribed. Smoking pot was a way of life in the 1970's and 1980's for us. Pot was very habit forming although we did not really think anything about it, was just a way of life at that point in time.

We would get bricks of pot and help break them up, and weighing scales were used to measure. Then we would sell bags of pot for $30.00 an ounce. It was fun and exciting; it was illegal though. We just did whatever we wanted. Why is that? At what point was it too late? Kids with no direction. Water finds the path of least resistance. Unattended children tend to find their own direction. We smoked it, sold it, grew it, we did acid, LSD, mushrooms, cocaine, and other experimental drugs. I took pills and wandered around. The worst was waking up on my grandma's couch naked and she was there. The other thing was at a friend's house and drinking a whole bottle of liquor and attacking a girl. It turned out horrible. That is where that big dog licked up vomit and got a bit intoxicated himself. I am sorry about that. I was drunk and threw up blood at the toilet the next day, about all day. My parents did not say much and did not take me to the doctor. They'd probably been arrested. I was only twelve or thirteen. It was the middle of 1974 I am pretty sure. If nothing else, please do not abuse alcohol, it will take a person to an early grave one way or another. I remember because the August Jam was coming and I was afraid my parents may not let me go because of that drunken weekend. I ended up going to the August Jam though, I forgot my ticket and left it at home, true story.

It was not a good day when one day I had to walk home from school, about thirteen miles. My friend said he'd walk with me, so he did. We made the hike and it was late. When I got up to the house, my dad came outside to get my friend off the property, blacks were not allowed at our home. I was so embarrassed. I guess I was supposed to know this through chitchat about African American people. I just did not know the depth of it though. He had to leave really quick and walk back. I asked if there was a chance, we could give him a ride back and that was a stupid question. From that point in time I understood the stance of my parents. The point was that our family leaned toward discrimination. Later in life it did not affect me too much. I have had relationships with people of different ethnicity, and I love them. That whole discrimination period was an awful experience.

Riots existed in the high school after the busing issue was somewhat resolved. There was a mix now, two ethnicities trying to coincide together. We always had some pot or other drugs. We would get to know the housing projects better and learn about the lives of our fellowmen. I never saw or participated in a riot. We had fights and bomb threats more often than anything else. The late 1960s and 1970s was another turning point, attempting to get away from segregation. I had my issues, although I believe my issues were not a white-black issue. I believe my issues were more from the neglect, abuse, and not being educated on social behavior. Some of my frustrations came out against blacks just as well as whites. I loved my African American friends. I could name some of them today. Some have passed away. Our generation was a turning point in society. My parents talked out loud about things not worth publishing. My mom was like that up to the day she passed. My wife was like "wow", a little stunned. It hurt to hear such things still after the turn of the century.

We had a family dog named Skip. One day a black deputy came down to haul one of us to jail. The dog was a pound dog, from the pound to the country. And out stepped this policeman. What do you think happened? The dog bit the cop, and blood came out. The dog got his way, and the cop got his way as he was driving off with one of us in the back of the police car. We always had dogs and cats, it seems, but those dogs from the pound were always mean.

Idle time often led to mischievous actions, that is an understatement. On different occasions we broke into our high school and middle school. In the middle school we turned the snakes loose. At the high school we took scales and other stuff that I don't think we had any great plans for. The greenhouse is where we went in from. Two brothers were in the building when a couple of deputies came cruising by. They stopped at the Agriculture greenhouse while I was in there. The deputies got out of the car and came to the door of the greenhouse. I was lying at the foot of the door inside. He pulled on it but I had locked it. My head was at the foot of the door and don't you know he pulled out his stuff and began to pee at the base of the door. The pee splatter was coming through the bottom two-inch gap and splattering me on the face. I could not move. He turned around and walked away. I finally got into the school and my brothers said I was white-as-a-sheet scared. Yes, I was scared. I almost went to a juvenile home right then and there. We got back to the VW and carried on like normal until my older brother in jail told on us so he could get out of jail. That was not good, one mixed up bunch of people for sure. Some would recognize this as a successful attempt at premeditated release, never heard of such.

Rare Earth was one of the first bands I ever saw live I believe. Earth, Wind & Fire was the main band. It was the early 1970's, and we went in to the concert. It was a concert for the African American people, it was Motown. Us whites went in, we did not go down to the floor. We sat up higher, when we entered and looked down, I will never forget it. All the Afros were so big it was like they were covering everything up. It looked like one big Afro from up high. I mean this may be exaggerated a bit, and illusion or hallucination, not sure exactly. I remember the hair though. You could see a little bit of color and clothing but mostly hair. This is not discriminatory, but it was just that most all of the Afros looked like they were touching each other. Afros were so big in the Soul Train Era. Rare Earth was so good. I love their music to this day. One moment that stuck in my mind is when Pete Rivera sat down behind that drum set and it all got quiet, all of a sudden, he shouted "Your love is fading". It was loud, clear and had a tinge of reverb, my goodness, then the music kicked in. Celebrate was good but man, that was some good sound by Rare Earth. That show was the start of a mighty run of concerts. All that music was educational, and the experiences with drugs and alcohol can't be taken away. So, we grew pot, smoked pot, sold pot, and practically ate pot. One thing was that down at the body shop, they would lace pot and when inhaled it would tranquilize your body. One time I smoked some right before going to work at Kroger, I could not drive. I was probably late. It took me an hour or two to get back down to earth. I would not recommend smoking regular old pot laced with anything. Smoking regular Columbian pot is good for the digestive tract. There is that one problem though, it is illegal. I kicked that habit about thirty years ago when I met my beautiful wife. I quit a lot of things and it took years for my head to clear. I used to pray to God to help me get past the euphoric stage. He did clear my head and my mind. I can think now and am focused. Redemption can come if a person can get past the lifestyle that prevents a godly life. God will renew your mind, he renewed mine.

That one night we were over at a party in Wingate N.C and I got into that bottle of bourbon. I remember physically attacking that girl in front of me because she was so pretty. It happened in front of others and they stopped me of course. Because of being out of touch with reality, it is a no-brainer to say that alcohol will alter a person's behavior in a big way. That is the night there was throw-up all over the stairwell and their dog licked up the vomit. It is not something easily forgotten, seeing that dog later and he was flat drunk from the alcohol in the vomit. That was a time when being so free-spirited was costly. I almost died, not to mention the victim's emotions, I am sorry about that. How many times in my life has death been so close? It is hard to fathom. Alcohol poisoning set in to a mild degree and it took me days to recoup. It is a wonder that I walk this planet today. God kept me here because he knew I would commit to my promise. The way out was treacherous sometimes. Some would say it was fun but it was dangerous. We continued to abuse alcohol occasionally but never became alcoholics, speaking for myself.

There were a lot of skateboarding accidents, bike accidents and probably hit in my head so many times it is a miracle I am sane. At Buff's funeral my whole right arm was skinned down from a bike accident. Before the funeral, in my Oldsmobile Starfire, I was driving down highway 74 toward the Pilot station to get gas. About a quarter mile before me the station had a gas pump that just blew up. Somebody had driven off with a gas nozzle in their tank. It was the most shocking thing I had ever seen. It was a time to remember, skinned up, my dad died and the gas station blew up right before my eyes. I went on by and didn't get gas for a while. That was a day to remember as well. We have to keep on pushing though, life does not stop just because we see tragedy and crazy things happening around us. I have learned to keep my eyes on Christ and not be distracted no matter what size the dilemma. God has it all under control. Transformation did not happen overnight though. What was needed was some spiritual engagement to be able to do good later through some social activation if that makes sense. Sometimes a person has to get out of the muck, get a new perspective and then return with a different philosophy to help others out. This relates to being a brother's keeper.

We just did everything. There was no one thing that had us addicted; it was everything, if that makes sense. One may say some of us may have given up our souls for it. One thing that was going on in or about this time was that I was having dreams about walking up on a plane crash. The dreams were so vivid. This was so impacted in my mind that one day I would see a plane crash site. It is just one of those things that God shows you in dreams and visions, no real meaning behind it at the time. You just sort of wonder, will this ever happen?

My oldest brother dropped me off at school one time and gave me a hit of acid right before I went in. I must've been fourteen or so. It was a strange day one time when experimenting with my friends epileptic medicine, and I think I slept for thirty hours. It messed me up pretty bad. That was not a good idea, do not try that at home. We would experiment a lot. The most fascinating drug was mushrooms. Mushrooms seem to be an easy method to take a trip and never leave the farm. Does anybody remember the song "wildwood weed"? Mushrooms are considered by some to be dangerous in an uncontrolled environment. It is not normal to do these kinds of things. I believe the mushrooms were not real harmful to us physically, sort of like marijuana although different for sure. Both are still illegal in Kentucky as of this writing.

When I worked at Judd's restaurant cleaning and bussing tables. Elvis came to town, Charlotte. It was a huge deal. Everybody knew it. A friend who worked there went with her sister. Seems to me anybody who saw him, it changed their lives. Elvis has some kind of spiritual connection. I did not see him but I know the reaction I saw from people who did. My wife saw Elvis perform live. It was a community event when Elvis came to town, evolving after Vietnam, drugs and rock 'n roll were just getting started good. It was different from any other show that came to town. It is funny how it even impacted people that did not even get to go. It was like he was an angel God sent here to share with us in human form. I know he wasn't but he was special. Some people say Elvis was full of the devil, I do not believe that. I found a roll of film somewhere and had it developed. It came out to be pictures of Elvis on stage. The outfit he had on in the pictures was on display at Graceland when we visited Memphis TN. I still have the pictures.

We got a call one night at home that one of my brothers was laid up in the hospital. A couple of them had snuck up on a college class and from the outside threw several dozen eggs in the big commercial fan in the window to spray the class with eggs. My brothers ran and some students chased them. My second oldest brother jumped a culvert and did not make it, he busted his knee cap up pretty bad and they caught him. He was laid up in the hospital for about eight weeks or so. It left permanent damage. I mean who would think of stuff like this? Who knows what they did and got away with it? This is the kind of stuff we only heard about because they got caught or we may know about stuff because we participated, sometimes not by choice. The eggs came from my grandpa's work, he worked at Tyson Chicken factory and always had a ton of eggs on-hand to eat and to throw, obviously.

Some of those stories were sickening, speaking of chicken. My oldest brother was rumored to have purposely put his little finger in a machine at Tyson Chicken and he lost it. He settled for Twenty-five or thirty thousand dollars. I did hear that he may have done it on purpose with a hidden motive in mind. Stuff like that did not surprise me. He dumped a mop bucket on a guard's head at the High Rise prison in Morganton N.C. He was stabbed in the eye with a fork. He got his teeth knocked out with a baseball bat and it was something different all the time. Yet, people in the community kept giving him chances with jobs and whatever else they could do to try

SWEET REDEMPTION

and help him get reestablished in the community. All failed in the late 1980's, he was killed.

A joke to a person one time was that if I could dig him up, I need to kick his rear end and put him back. It is just a joke, he paid a pretty good price for all those shenanigans and we are left to get past it, with God's help, we have. I declare that because of the misbehavior and the selfishness, there are messes left to clean up. We are also left behind to get past the hurt, the pain and the emotional roller coaster that remains after a life is snuffed out early because of misbehavior and carelessness. With God's help, we have moved on living with a testimony. We are looking ahead, not back. An early loss of life was not a good sacrifice. Sacrificing the potential of a successful life is not exactly a good thing in my opinion. The only reason to look back is to go back to Jesus and say "thanks" for what he has done for us. We thank Jesus for bringing us through. He has led us out of the desert into a promised land. We are using all the negative history from our lives to tell our testimony about how a person can overcome. Overcoming a bad hand that we may have been dealt as a child is a testimony to help other people do good. This is the only reason I am writing this book, to prove that we can overcome and turn out okay.

My brother next to me pulled away early in life. I think it was from his fall off that cliff and he about got killed. He would not say much after that incident. I have no idea about the demons he may have been fighting. He would just lay around waiting then he of course worked at Judd's. He then went to Hardees. He loved Hardee's, dedicated to making money. He met his first wife at Hardee's I believe. He had two kids and abandoned them after he got caught up in the ministry. I label it as bondage when the ministry bares down on a family in a negative way. What is funny is that he bought an orange Pinto the same orange as Hardee's. It was almost embarrassing to ride in it. I did though, every once in a while, we'd ride to school in it. He never said much, very strange person turned out from all the abuse and our dysfunctional home. I almost feel sorry for him. It was not all his fault though, in defense. We were dealt a messed-up hand as children. Like me though, decisions we make on our journey are ours to own. We'll be forgiven although we should consider the livelihood of others as we grow, not just ourselves. His original two kids have nothing to do with him but yet he is proclaiming the Word of God throughout. Some things just have to work out on their own. I wonder about the kids though; we are friends on Facebook. They hardly ever got to see any of our relatives. Later he married a different girl and sought a new life in the church more than his ex-wife and kids. Roots are important. To me he must have liked the attention he got in ministry and he actually attempted to preach one of my brother's funerals. I did not like the fact that it turned into an alter call. I may be bias though. Anyway, in my opinion after he divorced his wife and left the two children, he continued to stay in the ministry realm. The divorce certainly did not have to do with her having an affair. He totally neglected the two children, met somebody new, and seemed ashamed of his past family. In the bible, it reflects on this type behavior through the story of Eli. Placing more emphasis on colleagues than on your own family can cause lasting issues. Being an example at work does not rise above being an example at home. Some people get profession blind and people suffer. Meeting the expectations from an employer may become more important than meeting the expectations of a family. This is devastating to a generation when this happens and it cannot really be undone. Once the scars are made it is tough to get past the damage. When this happens in the field of ministry it tends to make children believe that "if that is God, then I don't want anything to do with it". This is not good. I just don't get it and the kids took years to try and figure life out due to this rejection. People don't know how to handle rejection and I have often stumbled on this dilemma. How can a person reject a wife and two kids, move on to another woman and have three or four more kids while rejecting the original two children? I may be naïve. I think there is a special place for a person like this and I call it wolves in sheep clothing? I realize there are two sides to every story. It was just this one side that I determined my opinion from, the rejection of two children. I just don't fully understand and this possibly is why I never wanted to have a child, wasn't sure enough for a bright future at the time and then chose to help my wife raise her two and reaping the blessings off sowing into their lives has been great. I get my opinion about rejection from the story of the cross. People do not do very well handling rejection. Christ struggled with rejection as well. We can learn from Christ's experience with rejection. He rose again. That about says it all.

We stumbled upon so much tragedy and heartache growing up because of the outlandish choices we made. One night a close friend was camping out with my older brother in some tents, and of course everybody was drinking and stuff. It got cold about four in the morning and one of the camper people went to get in the truck to get warm. He accidentally knocked the truck out of gear and it rolled over the tent. It was a closed casket funeral because the tire rolled over my friend's head. He was a dear friend of mine even though he was involved with owing me some money, they had taken pot from me and did not pay. At some point you have to let it go. I did go to the funeral in Fort Mill, the same town that Jim and Tammy Baker ran their ministry. This was a very strange time in my life, losing another friend.

Football on Sunday afternoon in the backyard, was a popular activity with us ten boys. I was the baby of course. One-time the second oldest neighbor was running down the middle of the field with the ball. I wondered if I could knock him down. He was six feet and 230 pounds. I was four feet five inches and 120 pounds, I bet. I took off running full stride and hit him full stride front to front. It about knocked me out. I knocked him down and I thought I hurt him, he laid there a minute, and everybody was astonished I'd do something that stupid. I sort of hid for a minute not knowing if he was going to kill me or not. We never forgot that. He didn't beat me up. The other incident was when I smacked my nose on my brother's forehead. I broke it in three places and had to be hospitalized for a few days. It was a bloody day. We loved Sunday afternoon football.

My brother Joey was sort of a bully type. He was the one brother that later departed us in life way too early due to some terrible decisions. He would steal from me and act like all is well. I think their thought pattern was that what is mine is theirs, but what theirs is not exactly mine. He stole a box of eight-tracks one time and it deeply bothered me. I worked hard at building collections of things because

I never had anything. I finally had to put a padlock on my closet. The other time I remember is that he was supposed to leave money in my car when I left the bag of pot for him and his friend Rick. They took the pot but did not leave the money. I do not mean this in a bad way, it was just the trash we had to deal with by dealing and trading illegally, a lot of scammers. It took me days to find them. He was such a bully and a liar. He tried to be a preacher one time but that did not work out very well either, him and his sidekick buddy are both deceased now which is not a good thing. They both had such potential. I remember when he put on the preaching facade, and if there was not enough money in the offering, he would pass offering again, sort of a joke. It was so fake, in my opinion. I mean I loved him although he was a seasoned scammer.

 We experimented with drugs for twenty-plus years and did a lot of acid, Quaaludes, and LSD. One time while at the August Jam in 1974 (I still have my ticket in a scrapbook), we jumped the fence on the third turn at the Charlotte motor speedway. Anyway, we took acid and I saw the angel of death who came to get me. Something was protecting me from going with him and it was not my brother who would not quit jerking his head and saying, "I can't stop." I was protected that day, although I say I met death up close, but it would not be my last encounter of course. The show of the night was Emerson Lake and Palmer. They put on a laser show that made people pass out from tripping on drugs. Keith Emerson had a piano that rose about thirty feet in the air with him strapped to it. The kicker was when it started flipping in circles forward while he was playing some "Brain salad surgery". Geez, that was the peak of some major ground breaking for the psychedelic era for me. People took their clothes off and police dogs were trampled to death. Either I was seeing things or I saw deceased dogs and I am quite sure it is the latter. Houses were burned down and several people were hauled out on stretchers. It was absolutely the craziest weekend in my life, we had a jar of peanut butter and no money. When we jumped the third turn wall the track was like forty-five degrees straight down and my middle brother slid on the asphalt on his rear end. When he stood up, the rear of his pants was pretty much gone. Makes me wonder where the word "asphalt" derived from exactly, just kidding. He had to walk around all weekend with no shirt on because he had to cover his rear end with his shirt. I got lost one time from them and when one of them found me sitting on a post passed out I remember. They slapped me so hard to bring me back too I didn't understand why they slapped me so hard. It brought me too though. It was just that we were so far out on the edge we did not really know what we were doing. It is amazing we made it, I bet we lost ten pounds apiece that weekend between the not eating and the drugs. There was a guy we named "teddy bear" that screamed "I want to hear some roc 'n roll" for four or five hours non-stop. It was a spectacle. We'd be like "you think he'll holler it again?" Sure enough, he kept on for hours yelling at the top of his voice. I mean it was flat madness, people making love and urine up an inch deep on the ground at the urinals. Unbelievable at the filth. The Allman Brothers were the headlining band to wrap it up. Greg Allman was so out of it that they could not even play. It seems they played for about thirty or forty-five minutes if that. Greg could not pull it off, they apologized and went on. It was not a huge deal at the time although if they had stepped up to the potential of their band it would have been a lot better. No complaints here, no room to talk. Most people were out of their minds to some degree. We were experiencing high times in the realm of an evolution in our country. They paged one of my brothers over the sound system at the August Jam and he was actually serving time in prison, explain that one. I don't know how many people lost their lives that weekend but it was one to remember for sure in 1974. It was one for the books. Foghat showed up and Black Oak Arkansas came, it was Hot Nasty.

    Some nights I would just hang out at home and wait to see who came home and when. Another one of those crazy stories was when my oldest brother came home one night and gave me a bracelet and said he got ahold of Peter Wolf's arm up at the J. Geils Band show and he had ripped it off his arm. I kept it a while but what do you do with something like that? It got lost or given away. When I think on some of the aggressive move's we made it is unbelievable. I was right up against the stage getting mashed and fighting for my spot at Ted Nugent and the mic fell and I grabbed it and yelled "rock 'n roll" as loud as I could over the stadium. The next day at school I asked a friend of mine did he hear me? He was like "was that you? I was like yeah, the mic fell right in front of my face, what would you have done? I was living life to the fullest.

We were down in Marshville N.C. one night at one of my brothers places where he was renting with a guy named Mike and the three of us jumped in the Volkswagen and took off to the Rumours show. Christine McVie was right in the middle of Songbird and I was about twenty feet from her on somebody's shoulders. Right when she hit a silent spot, I let one of those North Carolina rebel yells out so loud I believe she jumped. She looked at me from about twenty-five feet away and my shoulder length hair was blowing in the wind. Christine made eye contact with me and laughed like "what a wild buck? I have been in love ever since, with Songbird. Google the words sometime, totally amazing song. I love the fact God saved me and I can look back and ponder some of those special times, with his hand on me. I love Christine McVie and Fleetwood Mac including Buckingham and Nicks. It was one of my favorite concerts.

Rock 'n' roll was the huge go-to though. We just loved to rock 'n roll, lift weights and get high. We graduated into a sound design stereo and we would buy an album here and there. My oldest brother stole stacks of albums from stores. We would get high and listen to Billion-dollar babies while lifting weights. Again, we did not have heating and air. Flat country morning and night. We'd listen to every hook, sound and ping to figure out what it was. That is why I was so good at sound in my later years. We knew what to listen for. Grand Funk, J Geils Band and all the bands. Big Brother and the Holding Company was awesome. Then we knew Johnny Cash, Waylon and Patsy Cline. Kiss hit, Black Oak Arkansas, I loved Jim Dandy live. Remember Jay Thomas and the radio station Big Ways? We were living the dream. Aerosmith and Boston, sex drugs alcohol and rock 'n' roll. We paid a price, although, to us it was not worth laying down at the time, it was risky and fun at the same time. We were not really in control as much as we thought we were. Bad Company, Bachman Turner, we did a lot of good concerts for sure. Believe it or not it was very educational. Sometimes we would pass out, sometimes without even seeing the stars. Now those type incidents were not too educational. David Allan Coe, Jerry Lee, George Jones, seen them all. Jackson Browne is one I heard but did not see. I woke up at the entrance as everybody was leaving and Jackson Browne was singing "Stay". This is a true story. I woke my brother up and said "I think we missed it". He about got killed the next day, he never went to bed and got flung out of GTO behind Masons department store back there doing something they were not supposed to be doing. He got laid up six weeks in the hospital again, ludes and alcohol, what a mix.

We drove that Volkswagen to Winston Salem to see Aerosmith one night when we got a wild hair. We had no money and barely enough gas to get there. We scouted the outdoor stadium out and found that every twenty yards there was a policeman. We finally found a gap wide enough that we could run and jump the six-foot fence with barbed wire on the top of it. The police came after us and my middle brother had on a leather jacket that was stolen from Chess King at the South Park Mall. It hung on the barb wire on the top of the fence and he was hanging in it. The police arrived as he slid out of the jacket and came with us. The jacket hung there as we ran. My brother was like "my jacket!", we were hollering "let it go man, run!" We found entry and we had been scoping entry while Ram Jam was playing "black betty". After we got inside, it was rocking. Bob Seger had just exited and we stole a cooler full of PJ and headed for the stage. We boogied all night long with Steven Tyler. It was as awesome as it could get if you liked rock 'n roll. I do not want readers to be defeated by knowing where I started, and where I ended up. Where I ended up is from giving my heart to God. I am sharing events that led to sweet redemption after forty years. The point is the trying of faith and persistence in believing Gods word. His truth keeps marching on, just believe and have faith and you will find sweet redemption. I know I was protected by God. I believed although I did not know how to do good with a good conscious effort. There was no structure or pattern in my works at all. I was not standing firmly on a solid foundation. I had nobody there to teach me. I slowly grew into a personal relationship with Jesus is what happened. After many years I was completely filled with his spirit and grew accustomed to not much desire for the excitement in that scene anymore. It was a good thing. It was exciting although it was also a dead end.

At the time, I was living for the moment and it was stuff like going to the Bachman Turner Overdrive show. It was a great show. I remember that one and it was a warped night, taking something called blue heavens. We went to see Jerry Lee Lewis at the Palomino Club one night and I think I may have seen a glimpse of him but I heard him. It is almost embarrassing although my point is that a person can overcome if they'll believe in a relationship with Jesus who sticks closer than a brother, get it? It took me forty years to see clearly.

I have to tell my Gene Simmons's story, I was up front leaning on the stage with my elbows on the stage front. We saw KISS a lot. I love Paul Stanley. Gene Simmons spit blood on me at the show and I slapped his face and made him miss a lick, talk about reacting in the heat of a moment? This guy was seven feet tall with those heels on. It was a little intimidating. I loved to rock. Sitting in IHOP after the show with fake blood on my arm placed me on top of the world. We went to see Bad Company one night in Charlotte. Before the show we were just standing around in a circle. I don't know what I took, but my friend (ran over while sleeping in tent) caught me and saved me from busting my face on the concrete floor. I will say it again, Bad Company was one of the best rock shows I ever saw. They sounded just like the records with more. Kansas was there but could not compare with Bad Company. I was starting high school at or around about this year. Bad Company was one of the best live performances. The song "moving on" was my oldest brothers favorite song by them. Every time I hear it I think about him. It is funny how a song can stick in a persons mind forever.

Neil Young came in about 1976. My oldest brother elbowed his was up to the stage and as Neil was playing "hurricane" somebody pulled on my brother and a fight broke out. A circle developed as the two were fighting in front of Neil Young. My brother body slammed the guy and broke his leg. The police escorted my brother out with no shirt on. About twenty minutes later he ran through the turn styles and busted back down to the stage elbowing his way right back up to the front. We had a glorious time. I think I may have seen Neil

SWEET REDEMPTION

Young twice and he is very good. We do not discriminate, Neil was not a Southern Man. Some of the fighting, violence and embarrassment got old sometimes and it made me feel on edge like something bad could happen any day. It did happen in 1977 when somebody shot and killed my oldest brother, I expected it but it was still tough when it actually happened. I did hang out with him a lot, we went places like to see Jimmy Buffett, Dr. Hook and Pure Prairie League, good memories and crazy high times, had the tee-shirt.

Occasionally I would go see shows by myself if I could not find anybody to go with and one night I jumped in the car and took off to Charlotte. I was going to see Kris Kristofferson. After the show I met him outside and talked for about ten minutes or so. One thing he told me was that he said that I have a sweet spirit about me. I still have our picture together. Little stuff like that goes a long way with me.

We were watching Lynyrd Skynyrd one night and my brother threw a beer bottle at Artimus Pyle's drum set, the bottle was like in slow motion. The bottle went straight in the hole of the base drum no joke. It was unbelievable. Every time I hear of Artimus, I think of that beer bottle. Artimus looked at us like "you guys are crazy". I was glad it didn't hit him. Some of these times are just implanted in my mind such as Ronnie Van Zant standing right in front of me barefooted singing "Tuesday's gone". Other memories were "Call me the breeze" and "Searching". One night he swung that microphone stand around and hit Allen Collins in the back of the legs and about knocked him down, we were all just so messed up and I don't know what Ronnie was on but it was good times. I remember Ronnie Van Zant saying one time that he would go bare footed so he could feel the music better in his feet and it worked up through his body. He could feel it real good bare footed. I remembered this when I did sound in the ministry. One of the systems I built had huge subs under the stage and between the bass drum and the subwoofers, the stage would vibrate. It would almost move your clothes if you stood in front of the stage, on certain songs. I first learned this from Ronnie Van Zant. I love good sound.

My brother next to me ripped the scrub board away from Jim Dandy one night, we took that home. I wonder where it is today, have no idea but who could ever forget Jim Dandy. He bared down on that microphone and sang "Hot 'n Nasty". I mean you may have had to have been there, I don't know. It was good for the times. It was story after story of what happened here and what happened there. It was never ending, dangerous and fun. It is easy to lose life living on the edge for so very long.

My older brother was sort of schizophrenic ever since he took a bottle of Bufferin and had to have his stomach pumped. He was never the same after that stay in the hospital for a few days. Once when my second oldest brother put on a red white and blue American flag shirt of my oldest brothers, when he was seen, it was ripped right off his back. They fought and my mom tried to break it up. The second brother was pushed into a window and his arm went through it and it cut a major vein. Blood was shooting everywhere and he had to go to the hospital over a red white and blue polo shirt. Just another day in the life on Olive Branch Road, "new beginnings". So sad, no structure and totally nuts.

I wanted to work ever since I could push a mower for seven or eight dollars a yard or clean tables for a dollar an hour. Hardee's work was an employer after I worked at Judd's family restaurant. I was fifteen when I started Hardees. I turned sixteen there and moved on to the grocery business. I had to wear brown polyester pants and that orange colored shirt. There was a lot of grease. I was embarrassed to work there because I would see people I know sometimes. I always kept an eye out for this one girl hoping she would not see me. One day she showed up with her mom. I was embarrassed but after I could not hide, I acted stupid with another guy to gain her attention and make her see me. I did not know how to treat her, although I had a major crush on her. Social behavior was not my strong card. It is funny and sad in a way because I blew more than one opportunity with girls that I could have likely had a future with if I had of known how to act. I ended up okay though, just wandered around for forty years trying to get there. We still love the same people fifty years later and have never seen them again except on social media, if you're lucky enough to find them. It's not odd to remember them in a good way, it's just the love that God gives us, a gift is what the bible says about it.

A cracked pot cannot hold water. All the way up to about 1977 when my dad died, I would have to say that the odds of me being a cracked pot were pretty high. It was at this point that I concluded that nobody was ever going to do anything for me or give me anything. I am not complaining, it was the hand I was dealt. I quit junior varsity football, I cut my hair off and made a stab at it working at Food Lion grocery store. My grandma called it "Food Liner". We just laughed. I was good at making money, reliable and I was still crazy but knew God had a plan for my life. I could not see too clearly and was still a work in progress. I started repairing the cracks and struggled with becoming a man. I had no role model or mentor. I did lean on God to help protect me because I was still doing a lot of bad stuff. I was having fun not really hurting anybody but not really making the world a better place either. I decided to take the Distributive Education (business) class in the eleventh grade, I think it was. (DECA for short). I would occasionally talk to God while I worked, honored him. I would tell God that I was working for him and it brought me a lot of joy believing on this. Have you ever been verbally accused of smiling a lot? Joy actually over flows when it is true joy from our Lord Jesus. I am speaking from experience. Now I feel like this is actually the first chapter in our redemptive years.

Some of our school pictures are quite telling as they should be. I started growing my hair long in about the sixth grade. Before any of the other guy's ever did. By the time I was in the ninth grade my hair was shoulder length and pretty. I didn't have a life much and the only thing I ever did was play junior football and was good at it. Yes, I scored a touchdown or two as the slot back. I also played defense as a corner back, I was pretty good to play both offense and defense. The coach really jumped my bones when he learned I had quit to go to work, rightfully so. I felt bad. I had to work to make money. The team won the state championship that year I believe. If not, they were in the finals. Anyway, I grew my hair down past my shoulders from the fifth grade up until I got the job at Food Lion and being in front of customers, I cut my hair at the discretion of the manager. He promoted me immediately with more money and I appreciate that manager on Sunset Boulevard in Monroe, North Carolina. He was okay and a guy named Lane helped get that job at Food Lion. He knew about my past. The DECA class helped me and encouraged me to look into the business side of employment. I was scratching the surface of business.

People have to change for the better, I could not continue my evil ways forever. At this point in my life through a mutual friend I met a connection to Japan and Thailand. We smoked pot, hash and listened to music on high-quality stereo. We were smoking some of the best pot you could find. The drugs were coming in the mail. There were ties to the black market and smuggling. I lost one friend in Florida found face down in a pool. The whole time I was trying to keep life in balance. I could stay up all night and then go to work. Sometimes I would hate it when I had to lay down it was so much fun. I did have a gun put to my head one time over dealings. We had some of the wildest nights you could have and stay up all day. It was comical at some of the stuff we did. A policeman picked me up one night, we were laughing so hard, I don't know what happened, I ended up in the cruiser and he never searched me or anything. He drove me around asking a lot of questions and brought me back to the pad and let me go. I think the lady over the pad probably had some pull there in that small town, not sure exactly. I do not remember what we did, we laughed so hard, it was probably one of those laughs that last fifty years. I mean these were good times, we listened to the white album all the time. We also listed to The Wall. We knew that sound like it was engrained in our minds, Nakamichi was our equipment in the 1970's. It was a dark side of the market is all I can say. I quit going over there after I met my girlfriend. She had a big mouth and was not used to being around such drug activity. She helped me in one way but I lost a big part of my life, it may have been God pulling me back to save my life. There are a lot of things we don't know. We don't know what we don't know. That is a fact.

The year 1977 was the year my future wife gave birth the first time. Of course, I had not met her yet. She was struggling with her own issues and later I was dealing with my dad passing away and my mom took off with another man. I had a brother or two in prison and one left for the military. One got married and worked at Hardee's. I was on my own trying to find my place working at a grocery store figuring life out. I tried to live with my grandma after my mom had me practically put out. She hired a maintenance man named Ernie to remodel the house. I lived alone in that house for a while. One day he had the electric panel off and he was working on the electricity and I flipped the power on and shocked him really bad. It was awful. I was at the panel thinking if I flip this it could kill him. I flipped it and you have never heard such an awful scream. I laughed inside. I really did not care. That whole situation was the biggest mess I had ever seen. He got rid of my cats. In the end, it all panned out. All those people have passed now and here I am writing about sweet redemption. Life is so full of decisions every minute. I am telling you that when you relinquish yourself to God you will be fine in the end. I guarantee it. I moved out tried to find my way believing God would lead me and he did.

In and about that same timeframe in the seventies, I went to get my license. I had driven a bit beforehand. I was not nervous. When we did the driver's test, we had to go down a gravel road. I had driven down a lot of those in the back roads. We always followed the tracks. I did the same thing on my test. At the end I found out that a person is supposed to drive on the right-hand side of the road. The State Patrolman did not pass me, he made me come back. Some kind of stall tactic. When I went back, I did not have to retake the drivers part although I had to take the written part again. Anyway, I learned that day that when you're on a dirt road, stay to the right, don't do like everybody else and follow the tracks. Life is sort of that way too. This reminds me of how people tend to follow what other people have done. It is just like my story here, stick to the right. Don't follow the path of the people before you, it may land you into the same promised land. Choose the right path and you'll find redemption. When I passed my driver test and got on up into the tenth grade I started driving to school. Due to the fact I quit football and worked at the grocery store I could afford a car payment. My dad helped me to get my Starfire Oldsmobile in 1977. I had to pay for it. I got a few DUIs in that car. I escaped a lot of them too. It seemed I could not make it home without running in the ditch. One night I rolled it, drunker than I don't know what. I walked home and put it in the shop later. I kept on doing those things between sixteen and twenty looking for some kind of direction with no real good advice from anybody, no real punishment from my parents either because my dad had passed on and my mom left town.

I felt like I was moving on up in the business world from Hardee's. I had first moved up to the Atlantic & Pacific Tea Company grocery store when I turned sixteen. Then I moved up further in the Ralph Ketner Food Lion chain. I had always heard Bob Seger's brother George worked for them but I am not sure if that was true or not. I just thought it was neat because I had the eight track of Night Moves and Hollywood Nights stuffed into my eight track all the time unless the Live Bullet eight track was in the tape deck. One story about Food Lion is that we would throw damaged items in the dumpster if they were beyond repair. If we could tape up an item, we would mark it down and sell it in the reduced section. There was a twenty-five-pound bag of white flour that got damaged and it was beyond repair. I headed out the back door of Food Lion to throw it in the dumpster. When I looked in the dumpster, I noticed something moving. I thought, there is a racoon in there. I was going to dust him down with flour. I threw the big bag of flour in there and it was a dead hit. All of a sudden, a black man arose out of the bottom of the dumpster and the flour had busted all over him. He looked like the Abominable Snowman. It was the darndest thing you ever saw. The flour covered him from his hair down to his shoes and he was like "hold up". It was too late as I was closing the doors to the store. I was totally laughing and thinking that he just got bombed. I know that is not too exciting although, I just really loved the grocery business and made a good run at it. I always thought clearly to myself that I was working for God, not necessarily for anybody. This was way before I ever started reading and understanding the bible. I did have those fleshly traits though, especially beforehand at A & P. It looked like A&P was going out of business anyway. We were actually stealing groceries because you'd look at a price and hit the dollar signs and enter. We figured out to just not enter the amount and hit enter and it sounded like it was ringing up. Isn't that sad? We didn't need to be doing that but it became business as usual. Eventually we helped put it out of business. I hate that but hanging around the wrong crowd sometimes will hurt you. It was good experience and I met a lot of good people there. I had my Starfire and was off to bigger and better things at Food Lion, going to school and on my own at sixteen. I thought I had it pretty good but was really just an accident waiting to happen. I tried to keep it between the lines. I can't believe I lived through it all. The year 1979 was when I graduated, and it was hard to skip school and pass too. I locked one of my teachers in a closet one time, sold pot, had hair to my shoulders, and loved rock music. I was a free bird and barely passed English, but I was the second of five boys to walk that stage. One of my grandma's gave me a TV for graduation and it made me think that what we do now will be remembered by youngsters when they are in their old age. I never thought she did anything for me because she had favorites and I remember that I did get a TV out of the deal. I graduated and tried to go to college to draw social security because my dad died but that turned into a scam.

 We skipped school with different people when everybody got cars. Sometimes we'd just ride around all day and smoke pot and drink. Other times we'd meet at somebody's house and just hang out. It was strange that you'd get up, get ready, and go to school to just turn around and leave. It seemed we would miss up to twenty, thirty, and forty days of school. The system was not yet structured to eliminate such attendance problems. We did all that and still passed so we sort of had our cake and ate it too. It was a lot of fun and most of that kind of stuff was harmless except for we weren't learning anything by skipping school. We were too worried about having a good time and going against the grain. It seemed that we needed to be doing something wrong. I paid for it when I started college. I was not book smart yet.

 Timing is everything, sometimes we may wonder why things happen at a certain point in our lives. There are reasons that only God knows as things are taking place. After we look back, we realize a lot of the reasons as to why. We also find ourselves saying "thanks" to God not only for helping us through the valleys, we give thanks that it helps make us better people if we can recognize that we have to get past things and forgive. We must, to live out our redemptive years. That whole story about my mom taking off with another man after my dad died was a major point in my life. I had to grow up early at sixteen and seventeen but when this happened and she sent a maintenance man in to remodel the house, I had to get out. I could not get direction. My mom basically put me out at seventeen and eighteen years old. I had two brothers in prison, one in the army, one got married and had two kids and I ended up getting married. I gave in and married this girl. I knew I should not have done it. I was alone and ended up moving in with my grandma a few days before hooking up with this girl and her parents for years, pressure of the unknown. I liked her dad and was experimenting in some other things, learning another lifestyle. He taught me a lot about hard work. Before I met this girl I had moved in with grandma, she'd wait up at night for me to get home and I'd be lit most of the time. She'd want to cover me with blankets when I went to bed. It's called love in which I knew nothing about. So yes, I moved in with this girl and her parents. I was at another strange place in my life "unsettled" would be a good word. She was throwing sex all over me and I liked it but then again, it was uncomfortable. I ended up using her and actually moving in with her because it was a sense of security. The pressure from her family was tough. I knew I didn't want to get married. I was too young and uneducated. I had nobody to tell me to go with my inner gut. I could feel God telling me not to but the flesh gave in to money and sex. I had plenty of money by marrying but I knew it was a terrible mistake. I had issues in the beginning and she wanted to be serious and I really didn't. I got married in 1979 with no place to go. There were drugs and alcohol in this marriage, and she ended up a little loose on me and eventually I left. Too many drugs and I was getting sick of it. She did not stop. I stayed married and separated because I was at a crossroads of getting away from drugs and the people associated with the supply. After I got married the first time, money was plentiful. Funny how that works. I was not after the money. I was searching after peace, direction and to do good. We lived down off Wolf Pond Road for a few years in Monroe N.C. with the drugs, money and alcohol. It was an awful reason to play the game. It was setting me up for something I did not want. Before I got married a different girl had taken me to a prom and then this girl met me and ended up talking me into saying, "I do." I never did propose. I knew I shouldn't have and spelled my name wrong on the certificate on purpose to keep that void. I hope it worked. I didn't need to and did not want to be married. I don't do stress and I thought to shut them up I would say "I do" even though I was thinking "I don't". That's bad. They won that battle temporarily and it was not real great. I was quiet a lot because I was not sure and not very happy. It was my own decision making, no excuses. After the marriage it was like "oh my gosh, this is not the expected feeling". It was really on now and I felt a bit sick inside.

About this same time my grandma on my dad's side remarried at about seventy years old. She married a good man and I would visit and sit out under the tree with him and pick his brain. I learned a lot from him and he took care of my big dog after I moved on. One day Sebastian ate a rat she had caught out near the smoke house. My step-grandpa had put poison out to kill the rats. He did not know my dog catches animals on a daily basis or just did not think about it. Anyway, Sebastian suffered a little and then passed from being poisoned. It was so sad. I did not have any anguish against anybody, it was just one of those things. He apologized to me because he could tell that a piece of me had died. A couple more stories on Sebastian are that one day we were down at the lake exploring. I stumbled upon a really large snake with diamond shaped head. Sebastian warned me of the snake by making a ruckus. It was so big that she was even scared of it. I did not kill it. We moved on, I had to call her on because I was afraid that she would get bitten. It was likely a big rattlesnake, that thing was deadly. The other story is that we were exploring one day and I ended up inside a pasture with a thicket in it that we were trying to get through. All of a sudden, I heard a tremendous sound and it was a bull charging toward me. Sebastian ran in front on me and distracted the bull and the bull started chasing her. The dog practically saved my life. You better believe I gave her big hugs all that afternoon. It was one of the most fearful times I ever experienced just out exploring in the woods and down near the lake. We all have our dog stories. Those are some of mine. My Grandma and her new husband made a sweet couple and we were a lot alike. He saw some of the fish I pulled out of the lake. I used to take some of the fish up to the poor neighborhood and give them away to the less fortunate. One day I was up there in the street with a bucket of fish and a lady came and got one. Another lady came and got two. The lady that got one turned around and hollered really loud "you got TWO!" It stuck with me, every now and then that high pitch voice rings in my mind. I will never forget it that she thought the other lady took advantage of the great giveaway. I still take extra food up to the neighborhood and if there are a bunch of cars at a small house, I will take extras to them. The houses are usually loaded with children. It's just something I enjoy doing. My other grandmother worshipped the ground that my criminal brother walked on and gave him anything he asked for. She also tried to divide her estate fairly among all her kids and grandkids. She had told me that she was going to divide all her estate ten equal ways, that way nobody could say anything about anything being unfair. That changed once she got older and gave power of attorney to the two children. They restructured the whole plan even after her house was sold years later and I got exactly nothing and that's fine. I do not worry about such and do not harbor any bad thoughts. We deal with human beings and have to realize that God's ways are not exactly our ways. God replaces what is lost and stolen ten times over when we stand on His word. It is a promise. I borrowed $200.00 from her one time and she made sure I paid her back, quite comical as I look back now at how some of my family catered to my oldest brother. If I didn't laugh; I would probably be mad. My family was infamous about taking money, land, stuff that was coming down the pipeline to share. There was always a selfish hand in the pot. I saw this as a child and lived it out as I got older. I never did take opportunities that robbed others and never will either. I don't really need to. Jesus has me covered ten times over, guaranteed.

As I was writing about earlier, it seems that in the 1970's my older brother loved to take people hostage or kidnap so to speak. It was some kind of control issue. There was this one girl that he dated a little while and for some reason beat her up so bad my mom said her face looked like a hamburger meat, now that is sick. He kidnapped a department store manager. The justice system arrested two other people for the crime. They were brothers. Then my brother proceeded to write the Governor and ask about getting the brothers pardoned. They did indeed get pardoned and then when it came time for the trial my brother testified that he did not do it. He recanted. The case was covered by the national news media. My wife told me way later that she had seen the news cast on that case. My brother said the system was so upset with him that they pinned midnight burglary on him and he did get a stiff sentence. I do not believe he wasn't guilty of midnight burglary and I am 95% sure he kidnapped that manager. He told me he only got seven or eight dollars out of the manager. I believe a few years before that he took off with a girl to Florida, considered to be kidnapping. I vaguely remember my dad having to go to Florida and bring back the Mach 1 mustang. I won't mention her name. I think it is awful and we lived under that control with little parenting. That is exactly why he got shot and killed. He was going to control a situation after being in prison for twelve or fifteen years. The world changes and adapts. He did not survive change, and it was very, very sad to watch. I may have said it but when my oldest brother got out of prison he came around and had not adapted to the changes. He has a birthday in July and I believe it was within thirty days of him busting in that trailer and threatening a Lumbee Indian with some bird shot that he had purchased. It was about a month after the May race in Charlotte because I had given him tickets to the NASCAR race. He got arrested at the race and a policeman broke his arm with a billy club. It was just so sad to watch. Anyway, shots went off and my brother got shot two or three times with a shotgun by the Lumbee. The Indian boy beat his head in with the stock. The Bruce Springsteen cassette was still in his cassette player when we brought the car back home. I made that tape for him. It was tough and it brought me to my knees even though he abused us and treated us so mean. We still love people hoping one day they will change. He never did change and unless he got saved in the twinkling of and eye, he busted hell's gates wide open. He should not have been in Lumberton,

North Carolina. He had direction. It was just bad direction. It is like watching a fire burn and you can't get too close to put it out or you may get burnt or killed. We use wisdom and let God handle things. That is why we live to find redemption. There were girlfriends and there were friends who were mostly in it for the good times. Just like that one girl I met through my oldest brother who was twice my age and in today's society it would be a crime. I didn't see anything wrong with it at the time and it was all consensual. It went on a lot among us brothers and age was not a real issue. It's just one of those things back in the day of flower power and the 1970s people took off their clothes and had sex. It hasn't changed much, I imagine, although the laws are stricter now. That may be because there are more people now. I don't know, I agree with the fact that the predators are out there and they should be hemmed up but predators seemed to be few and far between back then or they just kept it quiet. Abuse was going on, although it was not talked about as much, I am sure. I mean we were witnessing abuse first hand right there in our own home. We had verbal, physical, sexual and emotional abuse in our family.

After the busing of students, I had met a good friend and we became very close. He did not come out of poverty although he was getting involved with drugs and he is the one that ended up dead in Florida. He was very close to me. One time we were smoking pot at his house when he kept a monkey, with a diaper. He let it lose to run around while we smoked pot with it. The monkey would pick at my toes because I wore sandals. It was very distracting and strange to me. We got so out of our minds I stuck my mouth around the bowl of the bong with hot seeds and pot burning, and I inhaled the fire and all. It burned me really bad and everybody just laughed. We were totally out of our minds, which brings to mind the Jackson Brown concert. My friend would have made it successfully if we had stricter rules as kids. He was like me; he just came and went as he pleased. It costs him his life. I had many close instances with death. God kept me around to do a great work and I am doing it today. Giving to the kingdom of God and praying daily for wisdom and understanding, I also got a college education. It took a while because we skipped school so much it slowed my mentality down even more on top of the abuse to my mind as an adolescent.

SWEET REDEMPTION

My middle brother joined the army at like seventeen or eighteen to get out. He did not have a high school diploma at the time. He got his GED and went in as a private. We lost track of him for many years, and we knew he would be fine. There was nothing we could do about it. We lost him to the military with a ticket out. He went in as an E-1 and came out twenty-two years later as a Chief Warrant Officer II. We lost the top two brothers to prisons and crime with a warped mind-set. Both were later shot and killed. The fourth child as I was mentioning earlier sort of shut himself off to Hardees and got married. He tried to be normal, although those buried demons came back to haunt him. I know he is only trying to make it in life. I feel terrible for his first two children though.

It was interesting to be in a position to observe the six paths in front of me. I was the seventh. My dad was an alcoholic with the mind-set of a third grader's anger problems. I tried saving the beer cans my dad drank. That lasted about a week because there was nowhere to put them all. He'd usually buy PBR by the case and drink all day. Liquor did not settle well with him, but I never in my life had seen so much beer consumed regularly. I swore I would never be dependent on alcohol. I am not. I taste a little here and there but by far stay away from it. I think it comes down to morals and ethics more than anything. It comes down to priorities. If you don't have the money, don't buy it. If you do have the money, be wise in your spending habits. I had a mom that was naive to stay in an abusive relationship and sought outside adventures from the marriage. I had a brother who turned out to be schizophrenic who'd just as soon like you as kill you. Of course, we had quick access to cigarettes being as both parents smoked. We stole cigs at probably eight or ten years old and started trying it. It was not good, hard on our fresh strong lungs. As stated before, pot was a normal way of life for us in the seventies. The seventies went out with evidence of the changes to come. I saw it coming plus I had just finished high school and it was time to figure out a new beginning heading into the eighties. There were challenges and more change to come.

1980's

We all make mistakes and I will try to explain myself without throwing anybody under the bus. I guess I could use a Seger line and say "I used her, she used me and neither one cared". I did, I used my first wife, but it would not have been a marriage if I would have had my way. I was struggling, being in that situation. I was young, stuck and knew it. Should I stay or should I go? I should have gone. In the meantime, Tanya had already had one baby in 1977 and now in 1980 having a boy. I was struggling; she was struggling. It was all about the timing. She had moved out to North Carolina from Nashville with her truck-driving husband, and I was stepping into a failed marriage. I did learn a lot about how to make money. Her dad taught me how to run a wood business, firewood was hot in 1980, it sold good. I worked in the firewood business and at Kroger full time. Pulling away from the dark side of life began in about 1984 or so. I was getting tired of living on the edge of death. I told my now ex-wife I was done with the people and tired of drugs. I knew it would take a minute, but it finally came down to saying that if we had to cross that bridge one more time then I was done. So yes, I was married going through the early eighties and then I got sick of the drugs and the people involved with them. Yes, I moved out after people were coming by when I was not there. It was sickening enough to end it, and I am actually glad because God brought me a clean Christian person that helped me straighten up. We did make the first marriage work for a few years. We just played around too much with the crowd in the drug scene. I ended up getting an apartment while she hung out with some of the people in that crowd of folks. I had been in the darker side of life for a long time and it was sort of new to her. Timing was likely the main issue that did not correlate. I was wanting out and she had just gotten in to the world of sex, drugs and alcohol. It was a kind of freedom but it was old to me and not to mention risky with a big price to pay. When I was done, I was done and it took me years to clear my head. I wondered if I could clear my head and bring back sanity. I did. I did it with God's help, and I have done well. I did not take anything that was not mine when getting out of the odd marriage. I still wonder about that spelling of my name on that certificate. When I set up the apartment, I only took stuff that was from my grandma and some accrued stuff from a few years previously. Of course, what I did take, my ex came over and vandalized what she could. It took a while to get past it. It was the right thing to do though, I went back over to see about the house, and there was a guy already moved in. The forgery of my name at Sears and me singing the deed over was painless as well as being away from the filth, drugs and that mentality. I don't mean this in a bad way, I just needed some spiritual engagement and did not know at the time what was needed. Balance was needed to be able to do what God's intentions were. I was now on my way to taper off alcohol and it wasn't going to be as easy as I thought. It was a start after a small delay. Again, I was following the lead of God. I had no direction from any kind of parental figure. It was totally the spirit of God in control of my life. It was all I needed though. I was done. I was wishy washy a couple of months and finally pulled the plug and joined the army to get away. I had met my future wife and stuck with her throughout my military career of four years from 1987 through 1991. A good southern Baptist Tennessee girl who cooked, worked and did not do drugs. I was probably the worst thing going for her, just kidding. We were really good friends then and still are.

In 1986, I visited my middle brother in Aberdeen Maryland. I just needed to get away because I was really struggling to pull out from the scene I had been in and did not really know how to. I thought it would be good to get away and think, spend time trying to figure out which path to take at this point in time. I remember this because the Challenger disaster happened that year. I was walking down the street in Aberdeen and saw the crash on a television in the window of a shop. I will never forget where I was when it crashed and burned. I proceeded down to Goldsboro, North Carolina, prison camp to visit my oldest brother after I left Aberdeen. He wanted me to bring him his scrapbook with all his baseball pictures and articles in it. Thirty years later I found a picture of Clyde King in my brother's Bible and googled Clyde. Clyde is from that area of North Carolina and my brother got a chance to try out for the Yankees training camp pro ball league through Clyde King. Clyde signed the picture and I keep it in my office. I never got the scrapbook of all my brother's heroics in baseball back, but it didn't matter too awful much, the devil had such a grip on his life, he never would've made it anyway. God gifted him and it all went haywire due to no direction. He could have made millions playing baseball with a little more firmness in his upbringing.

My grocery store run was going to have to end. I ended up working at Kroger for many years starting in Monroe, North Carolina and went to Matthews after Monroe shut down. I actually got to help open a new store in Rock Hill, South Carolina. I was moving up pretty good until I wanted to go into management and did not have any education except for a high school diploma. That played an important part with my decision in joining the military. It seemed that I did not want to be just a clerk for the rest of my life. I saw clerks and they were aged. It didn't make sense. I had to make a change and believed God to get me to a new point. The time was right and my new girlfriend agreed and we were going to try to stick together while I was in basic training. We did actually, got married and are still together. We have been together over thirty-five years now. In October of 1985, I ran my first ever 5K run for United Way. Somehow, I got involved with that. It wasn't a bad thing. I was actually searching and feeling an emotion of getting away from pot and alcohol. It helped me to think about whether or not I could try and build my brain back. It would take years before I could actually feel like I could think clearly and make good decisions. I started to go over to Piedmont High School there in Unionville, North Carolina and started running twenty laps at a time, I liked it. I never dreamed I would run thirteen Marathon's. This time in my life was crucial for the remainder of my life. I was starting at twenty-five years old and really still had no true direction and watching the end of the hippie generation. It was a good era, but it was pretty much over with. I was at a state of damage control so to speak. New direction was pivotal at this point.

By August of 1986, I had gotten to know Tanya pretty well and helped her get the cast off of her broken foot. Tanya was single now and that is a whole different story in itself. My first card to her was Easter of 1986, so, we met at Kroger in 1985. She actually broke her foot at Kroger. She got hit by an electric powered pallet jack. I had my own apartment, so one night I went over and she cooked fried chicken, green beans and I think potatoes. She says I ate like an animal. The big problem was that when I sunk my teeth into that chicken I was thinking, "Oh my gosh!" I thought what would it be like to have somebody that can cook? I gave it a long hard thought for about three years, we got married in 1989. It was major because she had two children from the previous marriage and I knew nothing about parenting—nothing. I knew a lot about things that don't work out very well, I can say that.

The kids needed a role model though, they had no dad around so we dated for a long time and went places. It was a win-win; everybody loved it. Later in 1987 Tanya and I started getting serious and would sneak off to the beach, we even went in October of 1987. It was a great time just hanging out as friends and wrapping up some stages in our lives we both preferred to get past. It seemed like we were good for each other by what we came out of. You've read about my upbringing and she had a twist in her beginning stages and was brought up in a middle-class family with good values and good morals. We balanced each other out both amazed at the character developed in each other. We worked at Kroger and took breaks together. We smoked, joked, and dated eventually. I helped her and she helped me for about a year or two before I raised my right hand and joined the military and got out of Kroger. We took the risk for change and it paid off after years. We were getting closer to redemption. I started venturing out with Tanya more and more and one day we stopped at the flea market to look around. Who do you think I saw? We ran into my older brother walking around with somebody. I told Tanya to go the other way. That is sad but true. I wanted to separate myself from the old ways. Tanya did not understand but she does now. My older brother had actually threatened to kill my ex-wife. When I talked to her about it, we were contemplating reporting the threat to the Sheriff's department and decided not to and try to de-escalate the situation by isolating ourselves for a little while. He attempted to burn our house down by leaving a cigarette burning on the floor after he left one day. We were asleep, I never told anybody that story. My brother was hard-hearted, schizophrenic and had no heart for the normal loving and caring person. I was one of the caring people I just didn't know how to love. When I found Tanya, I thought we could make it work. It has worked with God's mercy. One of the children had ear problems. Between us not knowing a lot and an onslaught of bills, I had been known to pawn an item or two to get by. I always went back and got the item though. We pawned her engagement ring a number of times. After I got her a nicer wedding set, I did let the original ring go for cash. I have no regrets about selling that ring. It was a Service Merchandise special. We never did get ahead until we arrived into the redemptive years. I was guilty of driving with no insurance a couple of months in the late eighties I have to admit. We just could not afford it.

Often, I needed time alone. I needed direction and most all the time I was looking up, still trying to shake my old self. I got away by myself one day to the beach to clear my mind and catch up on my sanity. I was going through divorce and deciding about being with a new mate. I ended up on the beach at a bar and drank several small bottles of bourbon, not a good idea. I stayed around the ocean for a while and then decided to drive home. I was in Florence, and the last thing I saw was a sign that said, "Friends don't let friends drive drunk." It was a skeleton shaking a fellow's hand. I rear-ended a vehicle at a stop light, and my head went through the windshield. Glass went into a pedestrian's eyes and they sued my insurance company. They took me from the hospital to the jail and my level was point two-four. God saved me that day and I know it. The police told me if I was ever found in South Carolina again that they would lock me up and bury the keys. I was practically banned from the State. Oh, what a feeling, I bailed out and made it home with bandages and all, it was terrible. My little truck was totaled so I bought a 1985 Z-28 Camaro.

I was contemplating a lot at this point in time going through a tremendous amount of change. One day I took my car to the shop for repairs and rode my ten-speed bike back home. When the car was ready, I hopped back on my bike to go pick it up. I was crossing a major intersection when a car came plowing through and rammed me head on. I flew over the handle bars and busted her windshield. I saw my life go before my eyes. I was okay. It stopped traffic for a while. I carried my bike to the Hardee's dumpster and called Tanya to give me a ride. While I was at the shop, I got a call from the police that I had left the scene of an accident. I went back, and it ended up that the lady did not have a driver's license. I ended up suing her because she was pressing charges against me for leaving the scene. I won and she paid me a few hundred dollars for my bike and trauma. The next day the beer guy at Kroger said he saw me get hit on the bicycle and he had to sit at the scene a long time while the traffic was stopped. I could not believe that. It was funny though. It was a learning curve for me. It was also another warning from God that my life could end any second. I know God was giving me all kinds of signs. I knew it. I knew God was trying to direct every step I was taking. It was my flesh that kept me in the ditches. Redemption would come though because I believed. It was tough trying to evolve from what I was to what I was to become. I was evolving into a transformer by the mercy and grace of God.

During the Kroger days, I loved it. I remember when I would take breaks with Tanya at Kroger. I would order cheese crackers and macaroni and cheese. We would eat, smoke and drink while conversing. We would talk and help each other through our issues, so neat to have had her as a friend. Tanya was very sensible to me and that is what I needed even though we did not have a lot of money, it worked and it made sense. We were hard workers and knew what we wanted and we could sense that we could make it in this old world if we would commit to it.

We took the kids to a swim park somewhere near Winston Salem, North Carolina. We had a good time. The waves were huge, one wave knocked everybody every which way and I got kicked in the temple. Back then, the waves were a lot bigger than I see now days. A temporary hit like that to the head allowed water to get in behind my eyes and it closed back sort of trapping water behind my eyes. It took about twenty-four hours and the water caused infection while I was stocking groceries at Kroger. I went blind in a matter of hours. This was the start of an adventure I would not wish on my worst enemy. It took me years to get past this to where I could have twenty-twenty vision again. I was actually 95 percent blind for a while. Of course, I could not drive and could not clean, go to the bathroom very easy or let alone work. I had to go back and find my mom and get help with rides to the doctor. After my sight gradually begin to get a little better I ended up with binocular vision and had already joined the army. What a turn of events. This was another warning from God. It was a tremendous test for Tanya and me. I was scheduled for basic training and had a prescription to stay in the dark and not let sunlight hit my eyes until further notice. I tried to drive but only went about thirty feet and backed up, I could not see hardly anything. It was just a thought.

Yes, I had signed up for the army, so this must've been Spring 1987. I was out of work for a couple of months and actually used my accident and health insurance to pay a car payment or two. The only time in my life I ever did that. I told my recruiter what happened, and they let me go in anyway. I still couldn't see very well by the time I went to basic training in August. It was a tough time, and I found out I may have to depend on people sometimes. I was living in sin, and it was likely a punishment for staying married to one woman while sleeping with another. I know I got married too young. Off I went to Fort Jackson South Carolina, the State where I was banned from because of driving while intoxicated.

Since I had already left my first marriage due to all the things I needed to exclude myself from in 1985 or so, I needed to get out of that marriage predicament and start to get a clear projected plan. It was risky and it was tough. I gave her most everything. I gave her most all the personal items and the deed. I did not want any of her money. She forged my name a time or two and I found that out after she didn't pay the bills. I had a forgiving heart and the one thing I did was draw money for being married in the military. After the ex-wife found that out, she quickly gave me a divorce. I think I got divorced on Friday and married on Monday because I had by then met my future wife. That is an exaggeration, although not far off. I met Tanya and fell in love with her and joined the army just to be honest. I did like drawing money from the army for being married and overseas pay later. I would do it again if I needed to, nothing wrong with incentives to serve our great country, it was a peace time tour. I desperately needed an education.

Here I was at twenty something and having to figure out this old world. I had to clear my mind and my senses up and get away from the filth that I had been around for so long. It was not going to happen overnight. God was protecting me from danger and I had people trying to get me saved and I do believe some of them were not right with God. I could preach back to ones who dared. They just didn't know this shy messed up kid actually had a close relationship with Jesus and it was probably my grandma on my dad's side that had been praying for me. I sowed into her life until I couldn't anymore. I already knew the scripture of sowing and reaping, it was just that I had not experienced the redemptive years yet. I had not walked in redemption yet. By the grace of God, it slowly starts to mold into something great over time.

In August of 1987, I was scheduled for basic training. When I went to the recruiter office to tell them I was half blind they were more concerned about the statistics. I left telling them I could not see really well and it will affect my basic training. I will never forget it. They just said to go in anyway. When I got in my car to leave, the biggest bolt of lightning came down from the sky and flashed loudly right in front of me. It was huge. It was God telling me that he was watching over me and that even though everything was a confusing mess, he was still here. I recognized it quite clearly and it messed me up for a couple of hours. That sign from God made me content in the decision to go in. That was a decisive moment. I said "okay Lord", it was decided. I was ready for the MEPS station.

In June, at about the same time or right after I signed up for Uncle Sam, we received the news that my oldest brother finally got killed. I knew it was coming, but when it happened, it still knocked me to my knees; part of me died. I lost my oldest brother to gunshot in 1987 or so and lost my Dad in 1978 I believe. My brother had been in prison so long that he did not adapt to how the world had changed since the 1970s. One day I met him on the road and he had a big bag of pot laying on his dash, he was driving about 40 miles per hour in a fifty-five. He was just enjoying his freedom and I understand that. I turned around to catch him and told him that times had changed, we just don't really do that anymore, we don't leave pot laying on the dash and drive down the road. I was like, this guy is not going to make it. I really wanted to help him but man it was risky. Stealing and lying were still in his game. He had done most everything from murder, kidnapping, armed robbery, arson, he was a known narc, dealing drugs, abuse of all kinds, and rape. I did not want my new love to meet him, and she did not. It was quite disheartening when my brother threatened to kill my ex-wife because she talked too much. He was slick, but God is in control and gave him numerous chances to change. He would not change, unless he got saved in the twinkling of an eye, I would think he went to hell. I don't know.

This is another reason we are in Kentucky. The history of my family sort of erased any fond memories of the country life I was born into and I am appreciative of Kentucky and understand the whole theory in a different way behind Daniel Boone exploring west. Daniel Boone was in our blood. Funny how God works, ending up in Daniel Boone territory. New beginnings are good, for us anyway, all the way from "Olive Branch". Daniel Boone blazed a path through North Carolina and Tennessee on his way to Kentucky as well.

As a child of God, I had been trying to change, and when my brother got shot and killed, it made it even more clear that I had to recover and rebuild my life. I grew quiet for two or three years as I went on into the army. My middle brother had already been in a while. It had been about ten years since we had lost my dad. A tiny pattern of deaths had started. My oldest brother experienced a death that was a cruel, harsh death. We got past it in our own ways. The end of the eighties was nearing and another new horizon was on the brink. We were ready to move on and let the past go. Tanya and I started building our relationship even more. I was trying to figure out how I was going to get my head clear and rebuild my brain cells or even if it was possible. I kept believing and tried a couple of churches, but the people were not trustworthy enough. I needed God to do it, we never did find a church to commit to. We would go but we just sort of hid in the benches and seats and left incognito. We were definitely not committed to a church lifestyle yet. We did not fit in, we were sinners, get it?

Tanya and I got married in Elizabethtown Kentucky during my tour at Ft. Knox and have been married ever since 1989. She is a good Baptist Tennessee girl and she has helped me defeat demons and be a nicer person. She also helped me in my studies about love. I needed that clean lifestyle to help me become the person I was capable of being. She is a big part of us receiving redemption through Christ. We felt weird because it was like we both had intuition and trust issues I guess we could say.

After the manslaughter in Lumberton in 1987, this instance sort of cemented in my subconscious mind that I was going to end my stint with alcohol and drugs. I was starting with the direction of getting the college money for an education. God knew my destiny. This put me at twenty-seven and twenty-eight years of praying and living out the hand I was dealt. It was a good transition time, and sometimes you know when you know. Tanya was a clean spiritual person who had a coupe little twist and turns herself. We, with God, could make it. We got along and actually needed each other. The kid's dad had left and I helped her get child support and we both worked together at Kroger until I shipped out. Once I went in the army to learn mechanic work, Tanya continued to work at Kroger, and when I got out of AIT and basic, the ARMY moved all of us to Kentucky.

In or around May of 1988 I arrived at Fort Knox. It was five hundred miles from my hometown, Monroe, North Carolina. On one hand it was the ticket out. On the other hand, it was strange being that far out on your own and having to figure life out. I was getting into Fort Knox to start this new life Tanya and I were trying to find. We weren't that close to God as far as being in a church but he knew when we were going, we were past a lot of the temptations that normally pull at people trying to establish a future. This was a far cry from my childhood, my messed-up marriage and the life of a Kroger stock boy. This was the start of a good thing. The only catch was that I was about twenty-six years old and was joining forces with a bunch of soldiers younger than I was. Redemption comes at its own pace.

When I was in basic training, I went out to the gun range. I could not see clearly but about fifty yards, I was about half blind. There was no use in even trying to qualify because there was no way. So when I was on the range in basic training shooting an M16, I would shoot other people's targets that were within the fifty-yard radius. I remember the soldier next to me looking and trying to decide if he should tell on me for knocking his targets down. He did not tell and he got forty out of forty with ammo left over. I hit thirteen out of forty and got a waiver on having an M16. I did not like cleaning weapons anyway and later ended up working a civil service job at Morale Support eight to five Monday through Friday in Alaska without a weapon and no physical training. There was no way I could qualify. I knew it. I chalked it up as a no-go before I even got started good. Three-hundred-yard targets? Forget it.

I enjoyed shooting all the different weapons and throwing a grenade but I could not see very well. I started going to the doctor on post and they eventually gave me some black frame glasses. I did well in basic except for the range. I got out of a lot of normal things that soldiers had to do. I was picked to work at Morale Support. They needed a 63-Bravo, (light-wheel vehicle mechanic). It was sort of a blessing because I learned more about mechanics down at the Morale Support shop in between Elmendorf Air Force base and Fort Richardson than I did on the 63 Bravo side of the army. I was pretty happy with my job. Mechanics is what I really wanted to learn and learned more at that position than being a day to day mechanic in the army. That was the good Lord showing me favor there working on boats and campers at the Morale Support division. Plus all the guys in Civil Service were awesome to work and train with.

One funny thing that happened in AIT is that when I left the barracks one day, my wife (then girlfriend) came to pick me up in my Z-28 Camaro. I left with her. Remember I was not supposed to be in South Carolina because of that wreck at the beach. Well, what do you know? I was speeding and a blue light came on. Tanya switched seats with me and took the ticket. I was AWOL and speeding in a state I was not allowed in. My fellow buddies covered for me in the army back at the barracks and I didn't get caught. It was a miracle. That was the only ticket Tanya ever had up to that point. When I was in basic, we had to train with some pugil-sticks. I got called up to fight in front of the whole Battalion. The Drill Sargent did not like the way I was fighting so he was going to demonstrate how to perform. He proceeded to get ready and I smacked him upside the head and tried to knock him down. He did not kill me but he let me know who was boss. I won my battle against my opponent and will always remember hitting that Drill. Everybody was surprised I hit him but I was trying to get the jump. I just jumped too early and he put me in my place, rightfully so. It all worked out and, in a few months, I got my mechanic certificate and was headed to Fort Knox, Kentucky. It was going to be big time decision making for a couple that had just met and was going to attempt to make it in this world with hardly any guidance or family. God was totally directing our steps and we were totally trusting Him who reigns.

This was the start of a great life. It just took time. What is funny is that the children would meet their future spouses and have three Kentucky children of their own. They know I did not know a thing about parenting. We have two bonus grandchildren from Kentucky as well. It is funny that we came out of North Carolina and Tennessee and now we have roots spread out here in Kentucky. I think it is fascinating that if we had not come to Kentucky, the three grandchildren would not be, and don't forget about the other two grandchildren!

The good thing about Kentucky was that we're only a couple of hours from Tanya's family in Nashville. I just needed to get a house and get her here. I wasn't divorced yet, but I eventually got the military to move our household to Vine Grove, Kentucky. I got a part-time job at Winn Dixie stocking and found a little house on Hemlock Street in Vine Grove. We were starting all over again in a new state. It was good, but change can be tumultuous. We settled, and Tanya got a job at a video store. We were also battling getting child support for the two children. Funny how that is so common place in divorce situations with children. God helped me to not have children in such a messed-up world. Obviously, he spared a child from torment because I would not have had a clue, just like my two brothers that ended up dead, I was unlearned and it was very hard adjusting to normal society. It's tough stuff although Tanya and I overcame by trusting and believing we could make it.

I was at Fort Knox for a year and received some training in phasing out the A1 jeep. The Humvee was introduced in 1989 or so and I got to work on those at Knox. I was also, a driver in the new Humvee. I drove a Warrant Officer around a lot. We lived in our little house in Vine Grove and the kids went to JT Alton school. We stayed there and attended church up until the turn of the century.

When we moved to 106 Hemlock Street in Vine Grove, Kentucky it was just me for a few days, and Tanya and the kids moved up later. The household was moved, and I did my army duties and worked at Winn Dixie. One of the children had some medical issues and of course there were braces to buy. Tanya got a good job at the video store and did very well there and the owner saw potential in her and helped us to get established in Kentucky. I eventually quit Winn Dixie, and we began our journey. After we fell into church in Radcliff, Kentucky, we helped form a Christian band with Tanya leading on piano and vocals. I did the sound and was quite good at it because I knew how to hear every ping, ting, and boom from listening to rock and roll so closely for twenty-five years. We got her a piano, and we became quite great, if I say so myself. Our son played drums and the daughter sung quite well along with the rest of the choir we had built.

Then one day in 1989 I finally got divorced after being separated for a very long time in my first marriage. After about four or five years of knowing Tanya, we got married. I was married the first time about nine years total. It wasn't long after that. We went to the justice of the peace, got married and we went back to work. It was like we were already married. Nothing really changed except for spiritually. We went to the square in Elizabethtown, Kentucky, and said I do. It was tough for both of us because we just didn't know. We had been together so long we felt like it was the right thing to do. We did not go on a honeymoon. We married and went on as normal. We tied the knot on May 5th 1989. Tanya and I continued to support each other and we bought our first home together out in Flaherty, Kentucky. It was a three-bedroom ranch on a half-acre. We had four wheelers, dogs and a lot of open country. Really it wasn't too bad.

I went to Alaska in September of 1989. I never dreamed I would get orders to Alaska. We had the two children and it was a big deal not to take them to Alaska. The situation was that we had forced child support through the clerk in North Carolina. At this time now the ex-husband didn't want them to go to Alaska. He did say that if we would drop child support they could go. It was very hard to leave Tanya and go but I had to. I really did love her a lot. I did my trip, and she stayed in Kentucky with the kids. It kind of put us in a box although I knew Alaska would be a rough go for Tanya and the kids, so we were okay. One thing about the military—it is hard on a marriage.

I went to Alaska for twenty-four months and the army paid our house payment. Tanya worked and I had my fun there. I made good money. I worked civil service because of my eye problems and learned mechanic skills on small boat engines, ski groomers, snow mobiles and other vehicles. There are some great people in Alaska. I picked up cigarettes and also drank vodka at nights. I was lucky I did not die. God kept me around for a reason. I never got an Article 15 in the military and received my DD 214 and then sought-after college money through the G.I. Bill.

Some nights away from Tanya and being out in the world was not a good risk. Some nights I would drink a fifth of vodka and drive back to the store to get another fifth. I would be so out of my mind I would not even know where I was. Sometimes I'd wake up and not know how I got to where I was. Sometimes I would disappear from my platoon for hours on end. A lot of people did not make it. God kept his hand on me and helped me through the valley of separation from my wife. That is one thing about the military I do not like. Some soldiers are not mature enough to handle the separation and turn to things they shouldn't during idle time. I was one of those.

I did not want to better myself. When we'd get tipsy, a few times we'd get in scuffles. There was this one friend from up north that I had. We would party and fight. He never did get me down, I always won. We would fight friendly. It was the toughness from my brother that used to wait on me to get off the bus to wrestle. My buddy and I would drink and fight quite a lot and believe it or not it all started about talking smack about the South. I forgot where he was from but it just clarified in my mind that people still have differences about North and South, especially after a case or two of beer. Alcohol made me aggressive for some reason, not normal. I just wanted to get through the tour to get the college money. I did it honorably. Don't get me wrong, I love my country. Even though it was peace time, separation from family was really tough.

A couple of stories about Alaska are; a boy had to stick his tongue to a pole in twenty below. Just like the movie. That was a story. A Puerto Rican boy saw a moose rack go by the window at the shop and yelled out "it's a giant crab", really? The moose racks were tremendous. I saw a mountain lion in The Yukon. I would take people that came up from New York City to see the moose, they would be scared to death. We saw grizzly bear, wolves and the beauty was spectacular. Alaska is awesome to say the least, with glaciers, whales, active volcanos and earthquakes. Rainbows were very memorable in Alaska. The beauty was spectacular in Alaska. Tanya came up to visit one time. She thought it was cold and it was in July.

About seven people I knew either died or got killed while I was in Alaska. Jeff was a friend of mine that worked with me as a cashier at the commissary. He got shot on the Highway just driving down the road. There is a documentary on TV about that. They found the shooter. Susan was a cashier there and she got pulled in the Copper River fishing. You are supposed to tie a rope around your waist and tie the rope to a tree because the fish are so big that they may pull you in once hooked. They found her body. A guy named James had an aneurism walking to the mailbox and died. Gina, a friend of mine, her hair fell out. The meat man died. There was so many people dying around me that I quit the commissary and took to myself for weeks. I went back to work there later because the money was so good but my life changed from that. I still say that commissary was built on ancient burial ground.

There was a lot of risk in Alaska, although some of things I did were a reflection from my unleashed childhood. I took a lot of risks, although again, God spared my life.

I don't know if this would be risk or fun but to not tell a couple of stories about the dogs and the mushers would not be right without them. When I would get out and explore the beautiful State of Alaska, sometimes I would walk and sometimes I would drive the jeep around. One day I was walking in these tracks, like a bike trail or maybe even a snow mobile trail I thought. It never dawned on me what was about to happen. I am from the south. All of a sudden, I heard this yelling and barking, sort of frightening to be honest. It was all quiet and peaceful moments right before this. I was like "what in the world?" Suddenly I turned around and a team of dogs pulling a musher was like twenty feet away on the trail I was square in the middle of enjoying the moment. The sides of the path was like three or four feet high in snow. I dove into the embankment in time as the musher passed by with all the yelping "pretty" dogs in a whiz. It was so sudden like, I was thinking "I just about got killed by a mushing pack". This may sound stupid but when a person is out of their element it really is risky being out of rhythm with your normal routine. I mean we did not have mushing dog teams in North Carolina. I had never seen that before. It was risky and fun. I witnessed part of the Iditarod while in Alaska. The State Fair was another opportunity as well as Denali. I enjoyed the State Fair and that is where I discovered that people in Alaska smoke marijuana in public. I smelled it and then scoped it out to see where the smell was coming from. Sure enough, there was a man sitting on a rest bench just enjoying the Fair smoking a marijuana stick. This was about 1989 or so. I was totally out of my zone. Being out of the zone with my sleeping habits costs me as well. The first night in Alaska I had to sleep on the top bunk in the barracks. About 1 o'clock in the morning I rolled off the bed and landed on a chair. The chair back busted up my ribs and I kept that one to myself. I have never told anybody that one even though later

I heard it is more common than I thought at the time. I was a little embarrassed that I fell off a top bunk.

The other story on the sled dogs is that I was heading back south in December 1991 up in or around the Yukon Territory in my Z-28. I was on a mission to make it back to Kentucky by Tanya's birthday. I got to a point to where I was so spent that I had to take a nap in the car. The heat had gone out in my car and it must have been forty below, no joke. I lit a candle and left the car running. I climbed inside my artic bag and commenced to take a well needed nap. I actually went to sleep. It is amazing how much heat a candle can put out. All of a sudden, I heard something that sounded like wolves. They were howling and barking and it sounded like they were like right at my car. I was scared to death. They were really close. I managed to rise up and look out the door and a tractor trailer had unloaded their mushing dogs to feed them and let them stretch I guess, not real sure. You should have heard them, it was the most noise you could imagine around my car. I wondered if they did it on purpose or what but I slowly climbed back behind the wheel. I made a peep hole in my windshield through the ice, inside ice and outside ice. The journey continued on through the Yukon. That was one of the craziest things that happened to me while in the great north woods. I did see a big cat and ran out of gas one time but had extra gas in a can because I had been told that I would probably run out of gas. When I would get out to relieve myself I was scared of everything, my mind was shot. I called Tanya one time and prayed over the phone. I got a little frostbite on one of my fingers due to a hole in one of my gloves. Surviving in that kind of extreme weather, it does not take much to get permanent damage. I was so frozen to the bone before I crossed over into Montana that when I went in a gas station and my body hit that heat, I started shaking uncontrollably. It was embarrassing. It took me forty-five minutes to adjust to room temperature. I was in bad shape. Once I got going again I thought it would get better across the border. I was wrong because an ice storm had swept across the central United States and it was a slow go all the way to the Mississippi River from Great Falls. It was a tough trip in December to say the least, with no heat in the car.

SWEET REDEMPTION

When I got to go up north I remember driving out toward Tacoma and Montana, I was a bit scared when I had to get gas a couple of times because I could see the gas station sometimes but to get to it, it was a really curvy trail. It may look like a quarter mile to the gas pump but may end up being a mile or more because of the curvy roads. It was weird because I had blond hair and blue eyes, totally out of my realm by myself in Indian nation. Sometimes your mind will mess with you. That is why it is a good idea to stay grounded in God. I remember going in one station near Little Big Horn where General Custer died. An Indian boy was sitting there stroking his knife on a sharpening block while a "beautiful" Indian girl took my money. I was like looking at him the whole time. I could have got the wrong change back and not even have known it. When you are out of gas you are out of gas, its just that simple. I love the west, it is beautiful country and the people are beautiful as well. Everybody needs to cross the great divide at some time in their life. It is really something to see. I continued my trip on out to Tacoma and loaded my Z-28 on a ferry to Alaska and I hopped a plane and set off for our future. When I picked up my car in Alaska, someone had stolen all my stuff out of it. It wasn't much but to lose my cowboy boots and fishing equipment made me think that I need to be a little more cautious now that I was out in the real world. I bought the fishing and hunting license in Alaska although I was so entailed in all the other adventures that I never did drop a line in the water. That is hard to believe but it is true. The whole idea was to get that college money and do whatever had to be done to set ourselves up for success by trusting God. Fishing was not a part of the plan, obviously.

When the Gulf War started in 1991, I was one of the last soldiers to go home because there was a freeze on ETS'ing. I did not have a weapon and my time was up. I went home on December 14th 1991. I drove from Alaska to Kentucky in blizzard conditions in a Z28 Camaro, about four thousand miles. God watched over me and that was a miracle in itself. I made it home in time for my wife's December 18 birthday. My wife was still at the video store. I showed up there unannounced. That was one of those kodak moments. It was a miracle in itself that I drove the four thousand miles or so and made it safely. It was a spiritual battle won, very dangerous. God is good to us.

The funny thing was that after all that time in Alaska, when I ETS'ed we ended up traveling in Central America doing a lot of mission work down there. I went from one extreme cycle of weather to the other. I had two years of duty in Alaska before I ETS'ed. We did not know a whole lot about religion when we started entering a new church. We were survivors who had potential and drive. When we hooked up with the power of God, we knew we had the answer. We made our way up the climb to figure out the blessings. We taught, received, and continued learning all we could about people and God. Tanya and I are both intuitive. We know we have that in common. We talked a lot, argued sometimes, but always stuck together through thick and thin. We needed each other to make each other complete. We eventually plateaued out at that church and moved on to start a church, The Rock.

We lived in Flaherty about ten years and did more mission work and I was employed at a factory after I worked at a rental place. I worked a little bit in civil service but factory work ended up being my transition after I got back from Alaska. We bought an Alaskan Malamute for our little family and Tanya brought her a buddy home to keep her company, his name was Mac, a shepherd.

The end of the 1980's was the beginning of actually seeing a vision of the promised land, only ten more years on this journey and I did not know it.

1990's

My contract time in the Army ended in December 1991. I drove from Anchorage to Kentucky. I am lucky I made it through that because when my heat went out it became "survival". I am not going to lie, I was out there, but God had a plan. Those candles were a life saver for sure. I continuously burned them, even while driving. The most exciting and scariest thing I saw was that mountain lion in the Yukon Territory. It came out to the edge of the road swooping its tail and stuff like it was looking for some action. I was the action, getting the heck out of there as fast as I could with my studded tires. There was a ton of wildlife spotted up in that area. An ice storm hit in the central United States at this time, and luckily, I had those studded tires. It was bad but I made it on Tanya's birthday and met her at her work, The Video Vault. The owner of the video store that Tanya worked at had taken her to Las Vegas in 1991, and she met a lot of movie stars. New movie productions and marketing was the idea behind it. VHS was popular during this time. I was in Alaska that whole year, although the next year in 1992 I got to go and meet a lot of movie stars. We have a lot of pictures and we also gained our experience on the slot machines and blackjack tables. Tanya was good at blackjack and her boss taught her how to play. I lost a lot on the slot machines and stuck to the quarter and dime machines at the end because I lost about $500. Later, I ended up doing some work for her boss in another business he owned. It was the rental store and I delivered, picked up and did some Mr. Rental collections work. One story about the rental / collection business is that one time there was this lady on Ft. Knox that had rented a washer and dryer. She was behind on her payment and I kept trying to get in touch with her and she would not pay. I finally drove out there and she would not answer the door. As I was headed back to the van I noticed the dryer was on and heat was coming out the dryer vent. I was thinking that she is running that dryer and will not respond to our calls. I took my shirt off and crammed it up in the dryer vent to stop the dryer from drying. It worked, sure enough she called the next day with a maintenance request for the dryer. I proceeded to look at the dryer and got my hand truck and loaded it up. She was like "will I get another?" I told her to call the shop and find out what we need to do to get her back in business. That is a true story. It was also in the beginning stages of my collection career. It was quite different from the military. I tried a little civil service work when I got out but I will be honest, I love and support military and would do it again but I am more a civilian type person and working civil service was not a happy place for me. I went to work at the rental place and then moved on to factory work in 1993. I think I started off around $25,000.00 which was pretty good. We bought a house and did church for eight years until we plateaued out and sold out on that church we used to support.

 We then proceeded with our lives as I adjusted to civilian life. We had four-wheelers bikes and all kinds of fun for a sleepy little country hick town in Vine Grove, Kentucky. We had a lot of four-wheeler accidents. Two in particular I remember, were amazing. I was coming down our street on a Kawasaki 250 Mojave ATV and I had a child on board. Her name was Sam. I was pumped, my wife and kids in the front yard and all. I was going probably about twenty miles per hour and this car cut right in front of me so he could make it in to his driveway. Well I hit the car, the ATV went tumbling and I went over, the baby went bouncing across the grass on her bottom just a bouncing. It was a smooth landing and about five bounces on her bottom. I got up and thought, oh no. She was fine, I was fine and the driver said he just did not see us, on the road. God protected us from danger, we could have been killed right there. The other story is of our son. We kept them in stock on four-wheelers. He was out in the field where we had a mud track, it was perfect except for a couple of poles that used to be a pasture fence. If you get going very fast you have to watch out for the poles on the perimeter. Well, don't you know, he was really flying around and I went on back to the house.

He was having fun. About twenty minutes later I get a shocking visit from him totally distraught. He said he stuck the ATV. He did not have any shoes on and the lens' were out of his glasses. We went down to the track and from a distance, I could see the four-wheeler up in the air. I was like "how is that four-wheeler up in the air?" On arrival I saw his shoes in the mud, the impact knocked his shoes off and the lens' out of the glasses. That was tremendous. Even more astonishing, when he hit that pole it leaned the pole over about thirty-five degrees. The ATV rode the pole up to the top of it and the top of the pole, somehow went up in a hole on the bottom of the ATV. The ATV was perfectly balanced about five feet up in the air on this pole. I laughed so hard, he had to tell me that it was not funny and his mom is going to be mad about those glasses. He was not right for a couple of day's. We somehow got the ATV off the pole, it was a Honda 200 cc automatic, red. I will never forget that story. There were a ton of four-wheeler and bike stories, like everybody else has theirs, we had a lot of accidents. God watched over us for sure. Those two were up there on the top of the list though. I trained the children on how to ride a motorcycle. I also taught them on manual shift automobiles. In case they were ever in a predicament to where they had to drive a manual shift, they should be able to just jump right in and go. The kids wanted to go to school in the city, so Tanya hauled them to city schools until one of them got their license. We bought them cars as they grew and they moved out as time went on. We spent ten years in Flaherty, Kentucky fulfilling and raising the children and getting them going. One of our children married the nephew by marriage of Tommy Shaw. I met Tommy when he came to town. I told him it was funny that I saw STYX back in Charlotte during their Grand Illusion days. No big deal, I just thought it was neat that our move to Kentucky generated a long- lasting relationship with Tommy's brother, till this day. They are good people. Our Grand-daughter is related by marriage only. It's just an odd note. We were learning a little about God from this half-baked church that did not have any education. It was a good strategy for us considering we were sort of half-baked too. We didn't have the most money in the world, but we paid our bills and never did lose our credit rating. It was like we were maintaining and it ended up being a long time. After the kids moved out, we started talking about making some major changes and we did. We did all the graduations and one of the children ended up having a child and we took the baby and his mom in for a couple of years. It was good but time for change, so here we are in Elizabethtown and we have a few Kentucky born grandbabies, amazing grace.

I smoked Newport's when I became a mechanic in Alaska. They were hard on me. I smoked for a couple of years up until I worked at the factory. Tanya smoked too. We ended up quitting together because we were both sneaking and both knew. It was hard but it was the right thing to do. We set our minds on making some money and trying to figure out a way to get ahead. We were both sort of screwed up by what we had come out of, more me than her. We had good intentions and it took a while, but we worked through issue after issue and finally ended up with some degree of trust. Trusting is something that proves itself over a long period of time. It may not work out but in this case through forgiveness and understanding we ended up trusting each other and that was a big deal.

I had a lot of mental battles once I got back in to Kentucky. Transition from military to civilian is not the easiest thing to conquer. It was not that bad but just enough to cause issues in a marriage. Stuff like working twelve hours a day and running on little sleep did not help. I was squeezing in college classes when I could and that was tough. There was a little bit of bondage doing sound for the church. It is easy to put too many irons in the fire. Keep life in balance. It was a strange feeling being in this world with no real family left, although having a good wife helped out a lot. We were doing the best we could raising two children that seemed to be disgruntled about coming out of a broken home. It was tough odds against all of us. It was one of those things in that era that people were still adjusting to. Dysfunctional homes were on the rise. With the church being a military church and the pastors with little education it did not help expedite our progress very fast. We were edging into trusting God completely in everything. We were in over our knees with our level of faith. It took a long time. It seemed to be more about money at that church. It was a strange setup we made, but it worked for about ten years and that was good. We maintained that long. I want to say that we were not going backwards although not moving ahead, some would argue that point. It got better after we plateaued and departed ways. One thing we had to adjust to was that we were not experienced in people giving to us. We learned how to accept gifts from people that wanted to bless us. A few times we found ourselves uncomfortable when someone wanted to bless us with a gift or maybe they wanted to buy our lunch. We learned to accept offers and gifts because a friend of ours told us to not turn down gifts and presents. The reason was that when a lot of people give, they are sowing seed. If we refuse to accept a gift, the rejection could rob that person of their blessing. I know that sounds odd but take for example if we wanted to sow a seed because we knew we would reap a great harvest off this particular seed. What if the person we wanted to sow into said "no", we don't want to take your gift? That would prevent us from sowing into the ground that we believed was the right ground, therefore we are robbed of that potential blessing. We had to learn this and we understand the philosophy.

Speaking of the strange bout with the church in the nineties. There was a family that had drive enough to build a building. The building was nice and we all know, the people are what makes the church. We helped in music and sowing. I don't want to slam the effort too awful hard, although this was a strange phase in our lives. The one thing that came out good was that we paid our mission trips and went to different Central America Countries. The love was not there. It was not good ground. After a while even a blind man can see the light. One lady that we knew in that phase of life was found dead in Louisville, that death was due to a whole different set of circumstances. It didn't have to do with church except for the fact that she was a friend we knew through the church and we'll never forget her. The whole thing was like a bad dream. I was so glad when the turn of the century came. The opportunity had come to move on. The timing was perfect, it was an urging from God, no doubt about it, like "Olive Branch" and new beginnings.

Flaherty was our little town in Kentucky. The children turned sixteen and eighteen. Graduations and growing up were going on, and it would not be long and the children would be gone. I always said when I married Tanya that one day it would be just us two left in the house together. It comes pretty fast. Once you get there though, it is like old times except for you should know more. We still had a lot to learn but there we were together, really for the first time by ourselves. We kept working and doing some odd and end mission work. It still seemed though that we just couldn't get over that hump. There was some kind of strain on our finances and we paid out tithes and offerings. It took a while, but we finally pulled the plug. We tried and believed but it just wasn't right. We finally moved on to higher ground at the beginning of the new century. That was the perfect time to start making a change, forty years for me.

In the nineties we started taking trips to Mexico to try to bring love and help pastors on the Texas Mexican borders near McAllen, Texas. We did church and stayed at a compound on the Texas side. We took groups down and familiarized us Kentucky folk with life in Mexico. It was very educational and a tiny bit risky, especially near Laredo. We ventured as far as Monterey. It was not easy work. It was not the toughest work either. It was good training ground to see if a person is cut out to do mission work. We paid our own ways and took the children a couple of times. We loved to hear the Latino people sing loud and in one accord. A few times it happened, a group of Mexican ladies would sing in one accord real loud at the top of their voices and if you just close your eyes, you could feel it down in your bones. It was almost like feeling their pain in the strength of their vocals, totally awesome spirit. The Holy Spirit would fall sometimes and we'd just have the time of our lives. We'd also do vacation Bible school for a week, interesting journey, educational indeed.

Now think back at where I came from and picture me doing mission work, it is unbelievable. We would have church sometimes with roosters standing in the windows and chickens running around in the church. One of the pastor's would blow a bull horn once the spirit got right and everybody went crazy, lot of fun in the Lord, and Pastor Paco.

We visited Rod Parsley's church a few times in the 1990s and attended a lot of services when Clint Brown was the music director, now that guy could rock the house. He was good. Rod Parsley was good too. We also visited some services at La SEA Ministries with Doctor Sumrall. We met Kenneth Copeland, and Benny Hinn was another I'll never forget. I had binocular vision for years after I left the military. I actually got out on medical with the honorable discharge. We were at a Benny Hinn conference one night in South Bend Indiana, and he said for our section to stand. The Holy Spirit knocked the whole section out practically. I was left standing and a heat came over my forehead and passed down my eyes and went out the back of my head. In a matter of seventy-two hours my eyes were healed and I was so excited I went to get an eye test and for the first time in years I had 20/20 vision. This is a true story. I only use readers now, nearing sixty years old, a miracle. There is no more blindness or seeing double. God healed my eyesight permanently, I declare it true. It is my miracle. I want it told.

So, I had started in a factory in the early nineties and worked there for ten years. I swore to myself not to work at the factory for more than ten years. I set a goal because I saw that a person can dwindle there life away like a robot and I knew my potential. It was just like the grocery business, if you did not move up whether it took education or not, you'd find yourself dwindling your life way like a repetitive robot. I was not going to do it. I felt like people get robbed when settling for less. Less is not more in all cases. I have asked elderly folks what they would change if they could to it all over again? A lot of them have said that they would take more risks. I have taken some risk in investments and God has always given us great direction. While working in the factory in 1998, I started off in college using the G.I. Bill and after that I received help from the factory reimbursement plan. I figured out to always work for a place that invest in your education. I never had student debt, never. There were some wild stories from working in a factory of three hundred people and about three or four African Americans. I used to make them laugh and wonder a lot because I was an outsider being from North Carolina and military. One day a boy was sitting there staring at me and I pulled out a can of tuna and opened it. He kept staring and I just stuck two fingers down in the meat and dipped it up to my mouth like an animal. He yelled out "he just ate that with his "FANGERS". Oh, help me lord, I laughed so hard inside I thought I was going to bust a gut. I did get busted for my southern nonsense talk at the factory. I don't remember exactly how it happened, anyway I got caught saying the word "wasper". My grandmother called wasp, "waspers". One boy at the factory would not let me live it down and my nickname became Wasper. It was hilarious he called me that. He called me Wasper for two or three years until he left the factory. I know where I am from, trust me. That's country. Kentucky is country but don't get them started about that night Duke beat Kentucky with that last second shot during March madness. I was on the factory floor when it happened, laughing inside. It is funny that people know where they were when this famous moment in history happened.

I had granted in my heart that by the time I was forty I would have that office job with my own desk. That is pretty much what happened because I went to work for the Hardin Country School Board not long after I walked out of the factory. I was working one day at the factory and it dawned on me that I had been there about ten years. I had sworn to myself that I was not going to be a factory worker all my life. I slowly took off my boots put them in my locker and walked out of there. The factory eventually shut down a couple of years later, so I know it was the right thing to do. Funny how God leads us out of the desert land. I was still in the desert although it was like fresh drinking water after striking a rock, it was faith in the desert land, forty years was almost gone.

While I was employed at the factory around 1997 or so, I received a call from somebody that I had lost another brother, due to gunshots. My sister-in-law who controlled my grandmother and put her in a home to die took the estate. She had my brother sign a life insurance policy for $200,000.00 with her being the primary beneficiary. She shot him six times. The step-daughter received the life insurance proceeds and they ended up keeping everything as it was. Except without my brother. She claimed the old domestic violence story. I struggled with this of course but God helped me. I had a clown skit to do that Sunday after the manslaughter and did the skit. I kept it quiet and then proceeded to the funeral in North

Carolina. My mom struggled with it too and never got over losing two children. This is another reason I got out of North Carolina. There was no good for me there and I am glad I am out. I am past all that murder and ravage. God has had his hand on me ever since field day back in elementary school. I still find it hard to believe that my sister-in-law shot him six times. I got a copy of the autopsy in 1997. The justice system let her out on some kind of manslaughter verdict. She said it was domestic violence which I won't argue but six times in the back? The system failed and I failed. I probably should have defended him but at the time I was so stunned and also aggravated about the two of them taking my grandma's estate and practically killing her I didn't really care at the time. My mind was not ready for such a shell shocker and neither was anybody else. The shooter had a history of shooting in the past. She also had some history with my older brother. These are terrible people and terrible acts. He had married the girl that my oldest brother had dated beforehand. She took over and controlled his life. She was unable to control my oldest brother, imagine that. They ended up moving in with my grandma on my dad's side and alienated themselves from our strung-out family. It was almost constant war between my mom and them. The two cons ended up with a POA and sold all my grandmother's land and personal belongings and kept all the money and put her in an old folks' home. We did not get anything. I would have liked to have had my grandmothers old 1965 white four-door Ford Fairlane. It did not have any options except for a big ashtray right in the middle of the dash. My brother sold it for $500.00 and I found the guy he sold it to but the buyer would not take into consideration the fact that my brother sold it without consulting with any of the immediate family. One day I told my brother that I would take $15,000 if he wanted to take it off his conscience. He said he'd have to ask his wife, but he thought he could do $5,000. I said no and for them to live with it, I can certainly live without it. I turned it over to God, and overtime she ended up shooting him six times. I believe most of the shots were in the back, he was running for his life, no joke. No hard feelings, but this is the way some people get turned on at the thought of money. He died, of course, and she has to live with it. Was it worth it? After my grandmother's death in the 1990's, the same brother had fraudulently sold some cemetery plots that were in my mom's name. When my mom later went to bury him in one of them, the cemetery had to reverse the deal and put him in one of them. I mean, who can think this stuff up? I know it was the cemetery's fault for not keeping their documents straight and in order, but who in their right mind could push an envelope to actually get the funds? Not to mention, should I tell the family I sold the plots? I am yet perplexed about how sorry people can turn out to be by not only hanging out with bad company but by making terrible moral decisions. This was one of my brothers. Another sad thing was the day I found out that my brother and his wife paid to have my grandmothers pond filled in. This pond was one of those sacred grounds so to speak. My ancestors fished this pond. This is where I learned how to fish, with cane poles. We learned about turtles, bass, and what us southerners called "brim". The cows used to get in it, the pony used to get in it. I mean there was so many memories. It was an awful day, the day I found out they filled it in so they could make it ready for a house to be built on. They sold it. I just don't have the heart to do some of the things greedy people do. This is why I am living out my years in the sweet redemption of my Lord Jesus. We had to get past it so we could receive the redemption God had for us. We have received in now. It is sweet.

    It seems to me that balance is key. A person has to take two steps forward and sometime those old roots sort of make you think that you may be taking a half a step back sometimes. Stay focused and keep moving though. Eventually you will be far enough away from the past that it cannot hurt you in any way. I guarantee it. Keep pushing on. While things like this were still lingering from our wild childhood, we were in the mosh pit at Ichthus in Wilmore, Kentucky in 1997. We used to load up the van and go rock out to Christian music for three days and stay at a hotel. My son 'n laws brother was jumping around in the mosh pit and lost a contact. He tried to stop the moshing to find his contact. It was absolutely hilarious on his knees trying to find a contact in a mosh pit with a hundred people jamming. Those stories will go on forever. The year 1997 I will never forget it. In 1998, Ichthus again, in Wilmore, Kentucky. I would take a small group of teenagers up there every year for about three years or so. I was starting to clean up my act pretty good in the late nineties. One time I grabbed an old blue tarp out of the building before we left and threw it in the van to take to mark our spot down near the stage. We had a 1991 Previa van we used. We had about seven or eight of us so we got there and rushed toward the stage area to claim our ground. I told the kids to stand back while I flung the blue tarp open to spread it out, sort of like Barney Fife. I flung it and a mouse had built a nest in the tarp among holes and oil stains on the tarp. It was rugged. That mouse took off through the crowd and people were like "watch out! there's a mouse." We finally settled down and rocked out with bands like MXPX and Sixpence None the Richer. Those are good transitional times that we were climbing and growing in God, pretty funny stories about Ichthus.

The year 1998 was when we traveled to Chahul in Central America. This is 2019, and we celebrated the twenty-year anniversary in November of 2018 of the DC 10 going down near Quetzaltenango, Guatemala. We were helping out with a medical mission. On the way down, in Texas I think it was, I had seen in the airport that a hurricane was headed our way, but nobody really paid any attention to it. Near the end of the medical mission trip we got stranded out in the jungle and we made it back to the compound on the second plane load. It was a guess shooting the plane through the clouds to land in a valley. On the third return flight, the plane hit the mountain when it veered through the clouds, and our medical team lost about eleven fellow volunteers that day. We had been stranded out in the jungle and had to make three trips to get everybody in. I was on the second plane and helped gas up the plane for the third flight. I was going to go back out with the pilot and co-pilot but they needed my cockpit seat because there were eighteen passengers to bring in; seven survived. One of my good friends was in my seat, and I found his foot when I arrived on the crash site. He wore Shaq shoes, and his foot was still in his shoe when I found it. I was one of the first Americans on the scene and found body parts and some of my friends dead. Eleven people died on that day. Some I knew very well and served side by side with in the mission field. Our great leader was one of them, and he was the head of Living Waters Teaching. This took me several years to get past, although it has been over twenty at this writing. God kept me here for a reason, that was probably one of the closest times I came to losing my life. I witnessed gore such as the body parts and I will not go into the details because it could get down right morbid with some of the stuff I saw. A couple of people that were in tact were still somewhat warm to the touch. I actually found myself saying "wake up". It was like a zone in warfare for real. We were on the front lines of warfare with principalities and we recognized it. The Indians had taken everything they could from the crash site. I do not hold that in my mind though. It was survival. It took me years to get past this, but with God's spirit and leading, I am okay now. Later on I realized that as a child I had dreamed of this moment. Dreams and visions come true sometimes. This was one of those. This is a true story and of course in the dream it was not specifically in Guatemala. It was just a plane crash such as this one. The 1990's sort of ended for me after the plane crash, I just patiently waited until God said "move" and I did after the turn of the century. What happened was it seemed that I was building a relationship with the crew that ran Living Waters and when our leader got killed it sort of forced me to remain on hold and wait. It took a couple of years for me to realize that the calling at that ministry was done and I moved on and waited on Tanya to hear from God about what he wanted her to do. We needed specific direction. We did a lot of work around Central America, we had met Clint Brown and did quite a good job with the band. We were all dressed up and nowhere to go as one pastor put it. The Beatles wrote a song about that, it is called "nowhere man". We went off in our own direction with God's lead and it was the best thing that we ever did. At this point we are right on the edge of redemption, the promised land and did not even know it.

During all the Central American mission trips we had so many successful and funny Stories too. We packed a whole sound system down to Bluefields Nicaragua for one of the medical campaigns. We set everything up one night and thousands came. I did the sound one night for the band and was doing quite well when a scorpion crawled out of a groove in the soundboard. The music was sounding good so I thought I would crank it up a little and I did. After a while, the pull from the system blew an electric transformer up for the whole town. I remember shoving the volume up when it blew. It was so dark after the electric blew that we could not see 5 inches in front of our faces. We had to end the preaching for the evening and we were just getting started good. We went back to the place we were staying and one of the tv's had caught on fire. The people did not get too excited about anything. The whole town was under a blackout. It was something all the time in the mission filed. It was risky although very educational. One day I was working with the eyeglasses and letting the Indian people just grab a pair and put them on to see if they helped any. This was somewhat rewarding because this one man came through and he had the cowboy hat and boots, rough you know. He did not speak English. He commenced to place glasses on and take them off and get another pair. This went on for like a long time. All of a sudden, he grabbed a pair that actually worked for him and he started yelling for joy, saying something. He was going off. The bottomline was that he could see! It was one of those episodic moments for me, it was like a miracle. I could relate for once I was blind and could not see. I love this experience. Another was, the lines sometimes were a mile or two. People would come to our medical campaigns from miles around and wait in line. We flew into strips where there would be wrecked planes and we slept in the jungle where rats would get on you at night when you were asleep. We saw tarantula spiders and scorpions were common to see. My wife liked to work with the dental team and there was this one Indian that came in and was saying to pull all his teeth, in a different dialect. They finally got him all settled down and he was erratic in communicating to pull all his teeth. When he opened up, my wife said he had one tooth. They all laughed because most of the staff did not realize that he meant to pull "all" the roots. They did. My wife actually got to pull teeth while in Central America. We laughed but you would have had to see the seriousness about pulling all the teeth. There was a time when I saw a five ton truck loaded with people and a boy fell off the back and rolled several times. He got up and chased down the truck and jumped back on like it was normal to fall off a crowded truck. Just weird things you may see in the mission field. I had a black friend and a lot of Mayans had never seen a person of color before. It was amusing to see the reaction of people when they would see my friend. Mission work was tough although a lot of people gave their hearts to God because of our efforts.

Life has only gotten better ever since that time. Different stages, different outcomes. We started off doing a little bit of ministry and helps in Mexico and missions on short trips. I had been at the factory long enough to where it was comfortable to take off and fly out of the country. We did church building and vacation Bible schools just across the border, and down into Progresso. We ventured farther into Nicaragua, Guatemala, and took some mighty risks to help with medical campaigns in the mid-nineties. Up until Hurricane Mitch, I did quit the traveling at that point, and my wife went back one more time, but I threw the towel in. November 1, 1998, is the date I have in my head. It took me several years to get past it. I will never forget the little Indian girl that led me to the crash site running through the jungle barefooted. I had to yell at her to slow down and I was a runner, she could flat run, and I thought I could run.

So now we're heading over to the other side. We are heading into the promised land so to speak. We did not even know we were heading into our redemptive years until we had been in the redemptive years for about twenty years. We didn't have a plan, God did. We are living out our redemptive years and there is no way we can go back. We are mentally stable; we are saved by the blood. We are prospering and healthy. We have the joy of the lord and the holy spirit has filled our vessels. Jesus sits at the right hand and we receive direction as we pray together, we anoint our feet, our hands and our ears. We stand on the word and are enjoying the harvest. We have sown, planted and watered. We are grateful for the blessings that drip off our fingertips as we help others now. One of the major keys that opened doors was the act of Tanya and I praying together daily, best thing that ever happened to us for sure. Pray together and stay together, it works. Enjoy the promises of God.

Redemptive years

Right at the turn of the century we had plateaued out with the leaders at that church. My wife was in agreement with me to go ahead and leave the church right after I decided on my own to leave for higher ground. The pastors actually wrote odd prophecies down and put notes in time capsules. To me this was a little demonic, and it came back on them later when one of their pastors was arrested and served prison time for having relations with underage girls. This stems from the head down, and the respecter of persons from leadership made me think a lot. My marriage had issues and it confused us enough that one or two times I got so aggravated I had a hard time controlling my flesh. The answer was to go to a higher level and once we got out everything has been fine. We were learning how to rise above the pointing of the finger and people wanting to control our lives. It was bad just to put it mildly. Sometimes a group can be like a wolf in sheep's clothing and this was the case at this controlling church. It was good training ground, although no place to invest in for a lifetime. One thing about that church is that if a person made a mistake, it was like a deer on the side of a mountain left high and dry. A person can give a helping hand to lift up a soul or kick a person while they are down. We can kick a person down or lift them up when trouble comes. It should be the latter. As I said the word "love" was never taught there, and after I left, I found that I needed to do a study. I had quit that factory job and took ninety days and studied the word about love. I needed my wife to decide if she was going to divorce me or come with me. No pressure from this side. The church wanted her to leave me. The preacher was crazy about my wife and did not give a cent for me. I just let God have it, and he showed Tanya the truth, and the truth set us free. Once we were released from that bondage, we were free, sold out and moved to Elizabethtown, Kentucky. That is exactly what we did. There is bondage in church, sometimes a person may not recognize bondage and may not know they are in bondage until they are out of it. Then they sense that a weight has been lifted off of them.

In 2001, my wife went through a lot of surgeries and is actually a cancer survivor. All through our thirty-five years, for a good portion of those years she has had to take different medications. This one medicine she took made her have anxiety and one day she could not get her breath. She lay on the bed not breathing and started turning very pale. I had to stay calm and think really quick. Should I call 911 or try to help? I do have a little experience in health care and military training so I thought to myself, I need to give her CPR. I actually breathed into my wife's mouth and was telling her to release while starting to push on her chest a little bit. She released and started breathing again, I have never seen anything like that before, it changed my life. That was as close as it gets to losing a loved one although God used me to help my wife to get back to normal and she is well today thank God.

About that same time period is when we moved to Elizabethtown, Kentucky. It was that time period, just after the turn of century that we rented an apartment and paid everything off. We started a church and later moved on to attend Evangel World Prayer Center in Louisville KY after handing the church off to a couple who still run it to this day. We had partnered with a couple out of Louisville to start The Rock. After handing it off, our lives have not been the same, sitting under Pastor Bob Rogers. We sowed a ton of seed and have moved in prosperity ever since, I have to admit.

In early 2018 I was down at a farm we bought and rolled the four-wheeler. I fell down in a culvert and hit my head on a rock and it knocked me delirious. I sat up in a split second and the 400 cc ATV came crashing down on top of my head. It brought me back to reality and it about killed me. It crushed my body from my neck to my stomach. It gave me a double concussion; I wasn't right for a month or two, some say I still am not exactly right. I am kidding. I immediately jumped up, rolled the ATV over and it started. I humped it back up to the farmhouse as fast as I could. I could feel tremendous pain inside of me. The ATV crushed me badly. I was very scared that I may have had internal bleeding. I called my wife and told her I got hurt and I would be on the bed when she got home. I did not go to the doctor although I should have. I broke several ribs and it took a year or more to recover and heal. This happened in February so even though I was in training to run my eleventh marathon I did not run that April. It was only the second year in the past ten years that I could not run due to injury. God saved my life that day, again. The Holy Spirit protects me all the time, amen.

    That same year one day I got to looking for my dog tags and after months of searching I found them in a tote of flea market junk. I took a picture of them to put on Facebook and when I saw the picture and my blood type, it is B positive. A person may be "A" positive although for all the negative types out there, just make lemonade out of it. I did not want anybody to be offended by this thought. It is just the way it dawned on me. It was just one of those things, inspirational things that happened. It is B positive blood in me and I have always tried to be positive. It clicked that it is all in the blood, my whole life is about being positive. What a better way to be energized than to be blessed with blood type b positive?

    As of 2019, I have learned a lot about who I am, some may say I have found myself. I don't really know what that means although I can say my name has changed. So, who did I find? Knowing my name is edifying. I recognize the change as being a good thing for me. It used to be my middle name up until I turned forty, there's the forty years again. I mean we can't argue the fact about wandering around forty years. I evolved again, transformed at forty is my thinking. I am not the old person I have written about in this book. I don't do the things he did, I laugh when I see opportunities to take advantage of others and really just laugh because it really is not an issue. I don't let it grow, I let it bleed to death and several things have blown away from me in the dust. In forty years after I got my desk job with the school board, everybody started calling me "James," my first name. It stuck through banking and is the new me. If somebody calls me "Dwayne," besides my wife, then I know they are old school.

Some people know the old James aka Dwayne. My new life friends call me James. James is biblical and there is a lot in my name. Even though my parents struggled raising us, I have to give credit, I am named after James Vernon Tomberlin out of Union County, North Carolina. I give God glory for my name; it is great that the name I am called by changed after forty years wandering around in the desert.

When a person is sexually abused, sex abuse does not always have to be physical damage. My dad was a pervert mentally. He was downright rude when staring. Yelling in the bedroom was so very common, her and him. We were under pressure and forced to do things that were not exactly good for a child and these odd requests created obstacles for us to have to get though. Our minds were sometimes crowed with stress from an unhealthy environment, to put it mildly. We had to figure a lot of things out on our own. How unfair is this? We were not going to not look. This messed me up for years as a child, and I did not like being under that power. I learned when I got older not to have any filth like this in our home. I don't want it to be found when I am gone. You will not find one naked picture in our kingdom. God does not like it, and it messes with people's minds. I would rather look at a person and pray that they have a great day rather than be thinking bad thoughts and staring like they are some piece of meat. God saved me; he saved my mind. It has been a great blessing to get past this level of mentality. I understand the physical versus the spiritual beauty. I have the strength to restrain myself from the bad thoughts that can enter a person's mind. This helps me in my walk to not be distracted. I recognize genuinely being kind and the meaning of real love through Christ.

We had a lot of pleasant experiences at concerts but one of my favorites is a night we went to see Heart in town in the 1970's. I loved Nancy Wilson playing and belting out tunes. I adored her. She kept looking back at me and I thought she may communicate somehow and at the end of a song I held out my hand and she walked over and placed her guitar pick in my hand. It was a big pick and shaped like a triangle and had her name on it. I loved it. In my redemptive years I gave that pick to a friend in Elizabethtown that struggled emotionally. He is a Heart fan and I gave it to his wife to give to him. I told her there was one stipulation and that was to tell him it was from God. God will save him. Only God can do it, later he got saved. I love this testimony. I know God uses me to get through to people. It just takes faith. This is a part of sweet redemption. Again, I call it sweet redemption. He will do it for you. I still see my old friend these days, he actually goes to the church that we helped start, The Rock.

David killed a lion. David killed a bear and was used to kill Goliath. As a child, God used me to overcome obstacles and toughen me up to do great and mighty things for the kingdom of God just by second nature. The obstacles and dilemmas were a training ground for what was to come. God has slayed the demons that have tempted me in my walk, he has protected me mightily. Now that I am past that stage, I am content and know that God pulled me through. He set me up for success. I have heard his voice and have acted on it. In return I have learned about the number one gift and it is love. He loves me and I love his people. I have seen the wickedness and he led me because I have been faithful. I have not been perfect but I have been faithful. One of the many reasons I want to share my story is because sweet redemption will come, it is a guarantee if we'll just believe, be patient, and hand our burdens over to him. Let him move and watch over you, do not worry, He has it, we have to let it go to him and believe. I am past all that. It doesn't take much to get past it when we trust God deeply in all we do. Redemption comes, trust me. It just takes time, forty years in this case.

So, I just kept working, talking to God, and trying to figure out my direction. It wasn't that tough. I had all the worldly things going on and seemed to be quite happy. It was just that fact that I didn't have any direction, so I told God I was just going to keep working and believing forward not knowing where I was headed exactly. My issue with getting married the first time was that I knew in my mind, but my flesh was being pushed by others. When that happens, you can feel the pit of your stomach move in a funny way. Your mind reads the feeling and wants to say something and a person should. I just couldn't say out loud that I didn't want to get married. I should have yelled it out although there was this void I needed filled and was not mature enough to realize God had me. I was ignorant in my faith.

If a person has to swallow a rotten apple, don't nibble at it is what one senior told me except for he did not refer it to be a rotten apple. Just swallow the pain and move on, this too shall pass. The new millennium brought us hope, new paths and new ideas about our future. God blessed us to be able to step it up and move to a higher level. It seemed big at the time, although we were so green and unlearned going into the kingdom of God that now it seems it wasn't that tough at all. The first day of the new millennium I was a changed man and I felt the pressure and bondages of church lifted off of me. This was a wakeup call and I did not know it. A person can place themselves in bondage by being a "must" needed person to carry on a church service. When I left, I felt the release from a ton of bondage and it felt good. It gave me time to actually spend with God instead of going through the motions of church and bondage in the church. Does anybody know what I am talking about? I heard from him and started slowly moving again. Fasting and praying we helped start The Rock Church. It was a good time in our lives as we ventured to new and higher ground. God had us in the palm of his hand. My wife got a part time job at a domestic violence shelter after we left that original church. She was employed full time at that church. Now she has been at the shelter for over twenty years. A lot of seed has been sown there. Tanya started off as a part time assistant. Today she is the Executive Director. It is a success and I am proud of Tanya for this accomplishment. There are so many success stories from past clients. Some don't make it of course although we do our best to help in any way we can.

Two grandchildren were born to us in 1999. We helped raise one for a couple of years and in the meantime left that church and started packing up to move to Elizabethtown, Kentucky. From late 1999 to 2002 it was a crossroads. We made some decisions through prayer and fasting and moved forward to higher and safer ground. The reason we were able to survive such change is because we both believe not only in each other, we believed and trusted God to help us to pay off our debts and start all over now that we had discarded our baggage. The baggage included a number of things plus too my wife had that bout with cancer and God helped us get through that detecting it early and getting it out. When the new century started settling in, so did we. It was great.

So, there we were in a tiny apartment in Elizabethtown, Kentucky. We handed off the church and paid off bills. We ventured from North Carolina to Kentucky. I was out of the military and now basically heading in a new direction in the education field. I was an assistant teacher in the education field, had an Associate degree already completed. One day I received a call about a job in banking. I had accidentally left my résumé out there on Monster.com and did not expect this call. My wife was getting through the surgeries, and our two-year old grandson had moved out with his mom to start their lives back over again. While she was separated from our son, she met somebody else and had a couple of girls. That matter is a whole story in itself about our two bonus grandchildren, it turned out okay. Anyway, I went in for the interview, and I actually liked the thought of working for a bank eight to five and not dealing with a classroom day to day. It was more of an individual effort. I took advantage of the opportunity. I have been in banking ever since. I was a little fretful about working around young females in the education field anyway because I was always scared that all it would have taken was an accusation or something to ruin a teaching career. I considered this factor when getting out of the education field. It helped me to make the decision about moving from education to business. I did not like the thought of a student making an accusation and having to deal with that. It was always a matter of having to be cautious when working around children and teens. I could not let my guard down at all.

I did a little bit of work at a boy's home, and I also took some part-time work at a behavioral health clinic. Some weekends I would work on the drug addiction and psyche ward with adults. With my experience and what I grew through as a child, I was very familiar with alcoholism and drug addiction. I was a great help and enjoyed learning about the pattern of drug addictions and alcoholism in this day and age compared to what I saw in the 1960's and 1970's. The boys' home was a little bit different though. The sexual misconduct of juveniles and things of that nature was new to me.

Tanya and I still owned a track of land out in our old home place that adjoined the house lot we had sold earlier. After joining Evangel, praying and believing, we finally sold the lot to help pay off our debt. That year was 2003, and we bought a house in September of that year in Elizabethtown. We were on our new journey now. The house was a fixer-upper. I started my new banking job. Tanya went back to work and we moved into the basement of our new home. We started our project to repair the home and start our lives all over, new beginnings for us. It is so sweet. That year I started a business of fixing things and named it QD's Repair. The reason it was named that is because one day my wife wanted me to fix the dryer. I bought the part and put it on and it worked. This happened in about an hour, and she said, "man, you fixed that quick." I said, "just call me Quick Dick." QD's born. I later registered my business as Quality and Delivery; it sounded better. That used to be an inside joke, not anymore.

After I started at the bank, I picked up mowing to be included in my new business. I bought a little mower and packed it around in a van and made some money at it. I started running more because my scheduling let me. Fasting was something that Evangel taught, so, I started fasting occasionally. All these things meshed together created a new lifestyle for me and it seemed to be working. We were making more money and seemed to be focused in a new direction leaving the past behind. Something else we started doing was praying together. My wife and I heard this from Pastor Bob Rogers. The first time was a little awkward although after that it was a feeling of transparency. Now we always pray together daily. If we are not together, I will call or text a prayer to have that covering for the entire day. It works for us. It will change your life I guarantee it. A person cannot really pray very well with their spouse when they may be hiding something, this is comical but it is true.

Fasting, running, school, mowing, and banking were what was on my slate in 2004. We were settled into our home God gave us for $125,000.00. It was a fixer-upper about a mile from my work. Tanya was moving up at the shelter for domestic violence victims from part time to full time employment. This was huge. We were sort of in a pattern now moving up, and that is what the Lord showed me at the turn of the century. The thing to do now was to maintain, learn, and pick the brains of people that knew banking. It was coming together, and I liked it. We went through some more health issues with Tanya, but by the grace of God we always triumphed. We broke through any prayers against us and somehow made it with flying colors. We paid our tithe and offerings and was living the American dream. Two people from broken homes had come together and made it by believing and standing on God's word. There was no stopping us now. It was a three-fold, Tanya, me and the Holy Spirit.

In about 2005 I started reading the Bible through for the first time and have continued doing so throughout the years, reading a chapter or two every day. This has enlightened my mind about the old and the new. Between reading, praying with my wife, paying tithe, and other things, we had begun to make a lot more money. Pastor Bob is a prosperity preacher and it has been good ground. Our daughter-in-law was struggling a bit after our son left her, and we were able to buy a house and let her live in it for a low monthly rent payment. She had three children at this point, and it was nice to be able to do this and help. As of now we still have the house and she is still paying that low rent. The key to this was getting on a different track with God and again moving up in our adventure and journey. The Lord moved closer to us because we chose to move closer to him. He is a faithful God. 2003 was a great year. Every seven years seems to be a year of blessing. 2010 was a great year. 2017 was a great year. We noticed a pattern in a seven year pattern of blessings.

Things were definitely on the up and up for us. I had the other brother who was gullible enough to reap the consequences of being shot in the back. The middle brother who must've suffered enough to finally get a ticket out through the army and leaves our family behind forever for greater, better and more prosperous adventures. And I understand all this. I see six roads and I am the seventh path. What do you want to do James? I was quick to see that the way of righteousness would be my path. I had to start by clearing my mind back, building myself back to health with Gods help. God blessed me. It is the major part of this story, faithfulness and then came redemption.

One day after Tanya and I got settled into our new two-story home in the city after our two-year apartment stay, one of the children came over to visit. It came up in conversation about how nice our new home is. The conversation continued on and I had to answer as to why we did not have this kind of a home when they were growing up? Well, I had never really spoken about my past to anyone except Tanya. I mean I really came out of nothing. We did not know how to attain such a lifestyle putting fires out just to keep from continuously getting burned. We did not have any college education, stability, experience nor a history of money making to any extent. Even if we did I could not say we would have been smart enough to attain a comfortable lifestyle for the children. The children do not understand "why" sometimes. All they see is what is and what was. It is not equal when comparing what was and what is now. We were in a state of heading for the promises when the children were young. The blessing is "now" and in the future for the grandkids and on down the line. The curse has been broken. Most all families that are successful had that one generation that said "enough is enough". That one person or couple can affect the lives of generations to come when they take hold of the future. It is good to do. Now the children get it, the grandchildren get it and I can actually see the vision coming to life, it has arrived. One of the grandchildren received a full ride to a local college. What a difference it makes when we change our ways and head in the right direction. It is likely to continue for generations to come.

I was hustling pretty good in 2006 to 2007. I had that Previa van that I had taken the seats out of and had some ramps to load and unload my mower and stuff. I was making a lot of money mowing and working full-time. One day I went around a curve, and I guess the gas can turned over in the back and I kept on going smelling gas. I made it to our cul-de-sac, and my wife and grandchild was waiting on me. When I hit the right turn signal, the electric juice hit that gas that had gotten on the wiring harness. I hit right turn and a bomb went off. It knocked me out for a second and blew the skin off my arm and my ear. The van was on fire in the cul-de-sac, I had a ton of equipment in the back. My wife and grandchild were looking out the front door with eyes as big as silver dollars. The firetrucks came and I took a hit on the taxes for my losses. It was stupid, but I am human. God watches over me, he saved me once again. I guess my point is that things happen. We have to keep pushing forward with a good attitude, (B-positive). It is not a perfect world although it really is not that bad either.

I have to say that this is just another example of how God protects me. It is somewhat a no-brainer that he has protected me in so many situations; it is almost too much to record. These are just some of my examples of how God may protect you if you'll just believe and trust Jesus and the Holy Spirit to lead and protect you. I love having the protection, sold out! Somebody this dangerous has to have divine intervention. Dave Gardner had a joke on one of his old albums that went something like; There was this guy driving in his car and wanted to speed up and said "don't' worry, I have Jesus riding with me". About that time, he shoved the shifter down into Race. He is still picking his teeth up off that console. The other guy said "you better let him ride with me before you kill him".

So, there we were in or around 2007 or something, school, banking, own business. I decided to run a marathon, self-trained and sticking to the Bible. I knew I could do it. I started running more, bought the shoes, clothes, diet was right, made it through the holidays, and in April of 2007, I ran it. I did well and have since ran twelve up to 2019. I took a break one year my wife knew I was hurt and would not let me run. It could hurt a person permanently. One guy died in Nashville running a marathon. I will look at running another one later. The 2019 marathon was cancelled due to the COVID 19. God has saved my knees, they're good. I am healthy as a horse. It has helped build my mind back and it helps to not be so distracted by things. I would recommend running or walking to anybody. Plus, it motivates others to do good; running is good, if able. The bible tells me to run my own race so I do.

I mentioned that every seventh year seems to be a year of harvest from all we've sown. I don't know if it was because we expected a great harvest or if it is because it is scriptural. The year 2010 was the seventh year, and 2003 was, an on an on. It seemed this was happening up to 2017. We bought a house to flip at the end of 2017. We made a lot of money off of it. We gave the biggest offering that we have ever given at one time. We also made enough on top of the offering that Tanya and I had the opportunity to go to Hawaii for ten days all paid for. Now that's a great God. We had made a commitment to God that if he would bless us tremendously that we would give a certain amount to God. It happened just that way. We made so much money in 2010 as well. We bought things and went on trips to Florida. We were tithing and paying offerings. My wife and I had been praying together, which was a major change. God blessed us like none other, considering what we came out of. We knew what was going on. We talked about it and prayed over the family. We were just plain out living in the covering of God now. What's the use in turning back? I mean we are not rich by no means although we do not struggle anymore. This to me is considered to be successful. I don't mean that in an egotistical way, I mean it in a spiritual sense. This pattern should continue from now on.

    I became friends with Tanya's dad even though we were two hours apart. He was a driven man who lived through two or three deceased wives. He always wore a suit, drove Lincolns, and ate out all the time. He had a business and handed it down to his son. He was a great dad for Tanya. That is all I can say about that is what Tanya said. Her dad sowed in their lives and mine. We joked around, ate, and watched golf together on T.V. We'd go to the Baptist Church there in Donaldson, Tennessee, and go through the motions of church. It was a great life he lived being a veteran of WWII. I am pretty sure her dad played on the Grand Ole Opry. It's these kinds of people I started surrounding myself with. It wasn't until after I cleared my head, went to college, and got a good stable business and job that God started bringing me people that I could learn from and actually depend on to be solid friends. I had none for forty years. One exception would be my grandma on my dad's side. Her second husband taught me some insight and wisdom as well. He always said "if a person can live with it then you should be able to live without it". I have never forgotten that. I have actually written this a time or two in this book.

Tanya and I raised two children, and everything went pretty good as far as death and tragedy being behind us now. The children never did experience any real tragedy and we never took them to many funerals of close relatives. It is funny because it seemed like I went to numerous funerals and visitations as a child. Maybe because they came from a broken home, I don't know. Maybe God was protecting them from the heartache and pain of death. It was hard on them when their dad left, they never got over it. Some children continue to chase after their father forever, and that is great. It relates to that "Father hunger" theory in a way. I just don't understand because my dad was an alcoholic, abusive individual that just went through the motions and we were embarrassed and somewhat shunned in the community. We grew to not care much, speaking for myself, because some of us thought it was pitiful to not make something of yourself. I did not experience a broken home growing up. I just pray somebody will get some good out of this book, this is my motive here. God says to write your story, here it is. I want this book to encourage and help people, not hurt them.

My mom was wild as a buck and mom passed away somewhere in 2013 or 2014 from cancer. She had a stroke and was coming out of it when they found cancer on her lungs. She said herself that she won't have surgery and take the chance of a collapsed lung and went on to be with the Lord. I helped her last husband get her off and on her way. We didn't have much support except her brother. Our family was so small it is tough when responsibility pulls at you, especially when you're five hundred miles away. She appointed me to help get the Will settled, and I did it honestly, not taking one dime that was not mine. Some of the family came out of woodwork and took some things unethically, although I only talked to God and my wife about that. I kept our children out of that ordeal. So again, my step-granddad always said, "If they can live with it, I can live without it". That is why it is important to talk to seniors. They have already been where we are now and where we are heading. I have to add that my mom saved my bong, for I found it hidden away after she passed away. I kept it as a reminder of what I came out of. I did not know what to think about my mom saving my bong. It was absolutely hilarious. I had to think, now if I keep this I may get in trouble. I took the risks. The old bong t is in the china cabinet as a reminder to me as to where I came from.

God had moved us on up to where he promised us that we would go, moved up from the plateau we had been on in the 1990's. In about 2013, in the later part of the year, we purchased a five-acre farm on a credit card for about $29,000.00. We worked and worked for it and still have that farm. It is our getaway destination, and some have stayed there. So now we have several houses and have some overflow as God promised. We continue to pay our tithe, fast, and I always pray with my wife and stay transparent. Is it perfect? Not quite, but it sure is close. It seems to get better as we venture through our fifties and sixties. We watch the pattern of prosperity by following the word of God clearly. God has gotten us through it all to include cancer. We're helping the less fortunate and leaning on him. He is always directing us. Jesus sticks closer than a brother, I guarantee it.

In June of 2014, I announced to my bank I was changing jobs after eleven-plus years as a collection officer. What happened was that our bank merged. I changed employers and went to a better bank. I could not stand the thought of working for an Indiana bank living in Kentucky. I went to a local bank, and they pretty much hired me on the spot once I got the interview. I wonder why. I know the stuff because I just sat in collections the whole time, learning and processing the fact that there will always be bankruptcies, death, divorce, and loss of jobs. Liquidation is ongoing, and from my past experience, I could empathize with issues, not letting it out that I have been there and done that, I have that tee-shirt too. I am still in it as of today and planning on to continue in this career until I retire. It isn't that bad once you learn the ropes and are able to help people out every now and then. One story in banking I will share is that I helped a guy through a bankruptcy and ended up later helping him to get loan. A long story short is that one day I came back in from lunch and a bottle of moonshine was sitting on my desk. I love KY! It is a cool state. It's the people. It's the bank, its Gods Country as Blake Shelton would say. Working at a bank helps tremendously with your personal finances. Working at a good bank leads to a great quality of life. Stick to what you know, mind your own business, work with your hands and be prosperous is the way I read it. Praying every day and asking God for direction is a key.

I moved my 401K and cut a lot of the ties over there at the other bank when I left because some people acted strange when I left. I mean, why wouldn't I leave? They ended up laying people off and actually got bought out again in a couple of years. God closes doors sometimes and opens up new opportunities for those who believe. This is part of the ability to overcome. My whole life I look down the road and try to choose the right path without being distracted. Stay focused on him and lean on him to guide your every footstep. There will be a lot of wrongs, although when you trust God, he always makes it better, he pays double for the trouble.

More than fifteen years after we left that church, the Spanish minister was arrested for inappropriate contact with a minor. When we went there, the feeling I got was divided when it came to respect for our marriage. I believe it starts from the head down. I worked closely with this perpetrator's wife in Central America in the Andes Mountains, and I had an uneasy feeling about her spouse. I let it go, and then the arrest came fifteen years later. It's funny how God may give a person intuition with a tiny voice or an in-your-face sign. Either way, sit back, give it to God, and let the principalities of warfare have at it. Stay focused and don't be distracted. Tomorrow will take care of itself; it is a promise. We won't ever go back over to that valley, although it was a good plateau for us. It is good for people at a certain stage and then move up, we moved on to higher ground. You ever feel like you just don't fit in? It's all in timing, move on at the right time.

We are enjoying where we are while we are on our way to where we are heading. We let the winds of change elevate us above the issues, the winds of change carry us to a higher level. I don't mean this in any way except for the point of not feeding into things that will pull us down. I call it running our own race.

I have fasted a lot not only for spiritual reasons but for cleansing reasons too. We fast every year for some period of time, one, three, or twenty-one days. One time I fasted solid food for forty-nine days. I will be honest and say on the last day I was actually being attacked in my mind. I remember I declared that forty-nine was my number. I was done. I was about to my limit and recognized it. We find we have it made in Christ. We stay in him. We pray for politicians and leaders of this great country and support our flag. We flow from season to season waiting on new growth, and it comes every year. We have our dry seasons, and it gets cold, although we huddle through it. We fall from higher places sometimes into the huddling position. New seasons are our support beam though. Tanya and I cherish the Spring season and on through new seasons as they come, if we did not adjust to change, we would have never gotten out of the desert. We embrace change and adjust accordingly without mumbling.

    One of the big things I appreciate by living right and doing good is that when my mom passed away, she entrusted me to liquidate her assets. This was huge, although it was a narrow decision because most were either dead or involved with other issues. My one brother had health issues and did not come to the funeral. The other deals with leaving his children and starting all over again with a new family. Trust is the thing. I sowed into her life and was as honest as they come when it comes to liquidation. We split everything, and everybody was happy. It is not that big of a deal to people that are normal, although we were not. One friend of mine that I have discussed some family matters with came up with a slogan for my family. "If it is not weird, it is not right". That pretty much nailed it down. The handling of the estate was an opportunity to express through actions, honesty, integrity and good moral's. It was done right with God's help. After my mom passed away I had the opportunity to pick over some of her belongings after her husband remarried and left the household to liquidate. He lived there a long time before he decided to move on. We are on good terms with him still. I will tell one story on him. When my mom had a stroke. She was laid up in the hospital barely able to talk. I asked my mom if she had a bible. Her husband said her bible was at home although the hospital lets the patients use those bibles that the Gilligan's bring around. My mom spoke up all of a sudden while we thought she was hampered, my mom spoke up very loudly "those people are not "Gilligan's", they ae called "Gideon's". I about lost it. There was some conversation too about being caught between a rock and a hard place, I believe he called it a "delimo". I was like "man, that is funny". Anyway, I was going through pictures and junk she collected. She was a borderline hoarder. I found a Christmas list from the sixties. It is hilarious. It seems that the older a child was, the more toys you got. The oldest son got about ten items or so, the second oldest got about eight items and so on all the way down to the baby. My list consisted of one or two items but it clearly shows my Christmas gift was going to be a Rapid. I had to google it. A Rapid is actually a cap pistol. There may have been something else on the list but it was so funny. They say I was spoiled. I don't know about being spoiled. I mean who would admit it anyway? I know I was embarrassed a couple of times wearing clothes that did not fit. The hand me downs never ended it seemed. That Christmas list blew my mind because it depended on where you were in line as to how much you got for Christmas. I got a Rapid and it must've been good is all I can say. One year my middle brother had real high hopes for Christmas and all he got was a stuffed Zebra. I send him a Zebra every once-in-a while USPS just to keep him grounded. I will never forget his face, absolutely hilarious, a zebra, stuffed.

In my mom's later years she openly admitted to running booze for a man that was pretty well known out of the Smokies. I never really thought about it until I was liquidating her household and found a bottle of moonshine from the man himself. This guy she was married to gave me some information about the moonshine story but all in all I don't know the real story about the bootlegger. I think my mom was always chasing some kind of excitement and did not find the real deal until she discovered that Jesus is the real deal. He then took her home not long after she was truly living a life for Christ. She lived an amazing story and I am proud we were on very good terms when she passed. This is important. I sometimes cannot believe the story on my life and the fact that I turned out okay, amazing grace is an understatement.

I graduated college at the end of 2018 with a Bachelor's degree in Business Management and a double Associates Degree and still striving to learn ethics and morals and implement them. Consequences is my thought, I sow good, and the consequences will be good. I refuse to let the darkness get a foothold in my life and my wife's life. We stay focused on Christ in all we do on a daily basis.

So here we are in Kentucky with my honorable discharge after we moved from North Carolina. We have books and books of pictures and concert ticket stubs from the '70s. I have seen so many deaths not only in the family but of others. I can't count them all. There are over two hundred hours on my transcripts. Hurricane Mitch came close to taking me and did take some. The drugs came close, and I have seen the angel of death. I was running wild at eight years old and vandalized an airplane and was placed on probation for ten years. My uncle saw Vietnam, and it was a time to remember. Marathons became an outlet and helped me wade through the muck. I was 95 percent blind at some point in my life. Having learned real estate, I have been blessed with making good decisions now, buying some, retaining some, and selling.

We have tithed for many years and have attended church regularly. The mental and physical abuse from my bloodline seems so farfetched, although it was a form of entrapment as a child. The alcohol was flowing like a river daily from the time I was a baby. Drugs were plentiful, from Quaaludes, acid, pot, and LSD. Pornography was around the house for children to see and deal with the best they could with no sexual education. The loneliness was tough, wanting and waiting on some sort of direction. Bicycle and car wrecks and living in the danger zone was a way of life, not even knowing how far I was out there. I know some bash the military ticket, although if I had to do it again, I would. It was a lifesaver for me, and I am proud to have done my tour and got out honorably. Knowing a skill and having college money to do something good with my life was a great thing. Also working at places that pay for college and maintaining zero student debt is key.

When love came to town is when our lives started to take a turn. Up until about the year 2000, we never really studied or talked about love. My wife had love in her upbringing, although we never let love show much outside our marriage because we did not know how. That would be a fault in our raising our own children, although it is never too late. I am speaking more of myself here. I studied Joyce Meyer books on love, prayed love, and started walking in love. I found no anguish, drama, or stress in love. I started to find out that God loved me through every situation. It was helping to make this world a better place, one person at a time. What I do now is take care of my wife and remain a pillar. Once rejected, now walking in love. I have never seen such rewards. Sweet redemption is an understatement. We own a little real estate and are looking at retirement, comfortably. We have a date to pay our mortgage off and we have one home that is paid for already. After reading what we came out of please acknowledge that all this came from abiding in prayer and believing with my wife.

I want to say that out of us ten boys growing up together, I want to say that I am one for sure that goes back and tells Jesus "thank you". Thank you for helping us and saving us. I could lie and so on and act like it was me. But no! It was not me. It was God, he directed me to do certain things outlined in this book and to stay away from certain people. I was directed to hang with certain people and to be positive. I asked and he has led me and blessed me. I took a 180 degree turn and I go back now to say thank you Lord. I know you are back there and I do not want to keep my back to you as I move forward. I recognize the story of the lepers. I acknowledge you and your presence is with me as I say "thanks". Thank you for this promised land and sweet redemption. I am one of ten that come back to you and say "thanks". I hope there are more, for some of us it is too late. Death comes in its own timing, I made it back to you Lord and report that "we are doing well thanks to you". We had the opportunity to go to Israel and walk where Jesus walked. I was baptized in the Jordan and swam in the Red Sea among other things. This is part of the redemption promise.

We still have our trials and tribulations because we are human. A couple of years ago we bought a new car after my wife pulled out in front of somebody and damaged our car. We fixed it up enough to sell it at an auction and bought a brand-new one. We had not made the first payment and a car pulled out in front of her and totaled it. We went right back to the dealer and got a better one of the same make. Toyota paid off the gap between book value and what was owed. I call things like this "hidden blessings". Stuff happens, although we don't dwell on what was. We look ahead and trust that God has our best interest in mind. We do because we gave our lives to him. It is not a perfect world. Just make wise and good decisions and hand issues over to him and trust and wait on him to show you that it was the right thing to do to let him drive and just enjoy the view from the passenger seat. Do not get distracted, I cannot emphasize this enough. Our family is heading in a brand-new direction for generations to come.

So here we are, sane, having a great life, and healthy. We serve in the Lord with all we have, and he is helping us every day. We mind our own business and stay focused on Jesus. We work with our hands and help the less fortunate. We learned to let things roll off our back and let God handle things we don't necessarily agree with, we let it go. We are living out our days in the palm of his hand and we are protected by his shadow. Life is good, and we enjoy the things he has given us and we don't abuse the temptation, although we do have fun. There is no turning back once a person has seen the mercy he has on us. We are not perfect, but we are really close to the one who is, and righteousness rubs off on us. We look forward to each day and thank God that we turned out okay. I tell people sometimes that my name is James, not Jesus. James is His brother. I am not perfect although we try to be like the one who is.

After all the trials and tribulations we remain under the realm of our God. We have given in to his ways, and he has blessed us back with peace, love, mercy and grace. There is no other way a person can go through such a path and come out okay and sane except by giving your life to God and let him steer the ship. I don't have any issues except for day-to-day foxes that try to nip at us, although with the wisdom God has given us, it is easy to recognize when the devil is trying to get a foothold. We just go daily to our refuge in him. It really is just that simple—stay in him. Protect it and look forward to time with God early every morning, noon and night. Talk to him and ask for answers. Answers come in his timing, and when they do, bow down and thank him. It is obvious he did it. Have a mentality to be thankful to him for small things as well as big things you definitely know came from him. He never gets tired of thankfulness. You will find yourself laughing and grinning at some of the things God will do. He is the God of surprise, that's for sure. I can tell story after story about funny things that God has done. Some I keep to myself and some I share. One day I was thinking I need to store some extra water in the basement of the farmhouse in case our water supply gets contaminated. This is the honest truth, one day I was headed to the farm and about ten cases of water had fallen off a vehicle. All these bottles of water were on the side of the road, it was my sign. Anyway, there are about ten cases of water in the basement at the farmhouse, no charge. Thank you. I had only shared that story with my wife until now. That is hilarious.

May I boast now? Somehow God gave me the wisdom to recognize his spirit as a young lad. I trusted even though I could not see. I felt his companionship as I could not touch him. I heard his voice inside urging me to trust him, although I could not locate a being. I felt his comfort fifty years ago, and I feel his comfort in these redemption days. The pattern of my life simply shows that he has taken care of me through this rough and treacherous hand I was dealt as a child. My mind is clear, and I am not scared or fearful in the least bit. As a matter of fact, with the history of street experience, the Word of God and my education, I turned out what I call successful comparing to the pyramid of success. If I had not been dealt that hand, who is to say where I would be today? I know I overcame by the blood of the Lamb and turned out successful. This is my testimony.

Some are born with a lead from their parents. I don't have any issues with that. The thing is, somewhere up that line, there was somebody with nothing to start with, and they did the same thing I have done, through Christ Jesus. I guarantee it. I have arrived at a point to where I do not feel like I am owed anything. This may relate to Maslow's hierarchy of needs. What was lost as a child took a turn. There was a turning point. There is no chip on my shoulder for God carried the weight. I am not on the defensive in wanting things my way. A love arose inside of me because I realized I have been paid back a hundred-fold for all that was lost and stolen. Lost is an interesting word. Found is more interesting because it creates excitement in our attitude. To be found, to find and discover creates a special and lasting joy that can only come from God.

Wrapping this up, my final word is that when a person sees God and believes, at that point things start to change. Wisdom and understanding start to creep into your mind and soul; favor will come and don't ever give up. It may not happen overnight. In my case it took me forty years to get to this destination. Are times perfect? Not perfect but really close because I don't carry the yoke. He does. Live and make this world a better place. Do what you are called to do. Love and mind your own business. Use your mind, feet, and hands to carry out your calling. Be a listener for his voice and act accordingly. I remember sending Jane that book in the mail and later on she passed away, about a year later, That is what I am talking about. I did not know if she needed that book or not, listen. He has us in his palm, under his arm of protection. Don't carry the weight. He is strong enough to carry the world. He can certainly carry you. Abide in the laws of this wonderful land. Cherish our freedom and our freedom in Christ.

Finally, in closing, I want to thank God for saving and protecting me. I pray that as my two brothers died of gunshot wounds, they got saved in the twinkling of an eye. I pray for the survivors of the plane crash and the family of the victims in the crash. I pray this tragedy will not haunt anyone on the anniversary date each year. and that God's name be glorified through the understanding of principalities and spiritual warfare. I thank God for helping me build back my brain and that I have common logic to combine street-smart and education to be self-actualized. Thank you, God, for allowing me to overcome blindness and be a testimony of healing. Thank you, God, for great genes and good health. Thank you for my wife for being hard on me to make me a better and stronger person, a survivor in you. We know it's funny that for forty years my name plate was my middle name. After I started as the assistant schoolteacher in 2001 or so and then continued into banking my name became my first name. My new name at the beginning of Sweet Redemption became my name to be called by. My first name has been my real name ever since, "James." The Lord gives names. Left alone God changed my called name. I have become a transformer, a transformation has taken place, this is my real identity. Who am I? My real identity is James. This change took place forty years after I was born, I guess you could say I was reborn. My goal now is to make positive changes in the world while waiting on heaven to come, from Olive Branch Road comes "new beginnings". Sweet redemption started about the same month I was born, early fall of 2001 it was almost to the day of being forty years. I am a walking miracle, not perfect, close to the one who is. We are living the good life here on earth and I call it Sweet Redemption-blessings! It is good, thank you Lord for sweet redemption. It was well worth giving my life to you, being reborn and being able to share My story. We enter this world, exit and live eternally with God if we'll just stand on His word and believe - blessings from God to you, amen!

About the Author

From the perspective of the baby of five boys born into this world with little direction, analyzing the paths of a family that were less than desirable, questions and commitments to God are verbalized. Through the painful and agonizing twists and turns in life, God sticks closer than a brother and leads a young boy out of temptation and evil. After forty years, he finds his place in God's kingdom and realizes that God is truly faithful and that sweet redemption comes to those who believe and we are proof of his promises.

Contact information: tamesta@bbtel.com